MARTINA'S KITCHEN MIX

∽My Recipe Playlist for Real Life∽

MARTINA'S KITCHEN MIX

~My Recipe Playlist for Real Life~

Martina McBride

Oxmoor
HOUSE®

Design and Photography ©2018 Time Inc. Books,
a division of Meredith Corporation
Published by Oxmoor House,
an imprint of Time Inc. Books
225 Liberty Street, New York, NY 10281

Executive Editor: Katherine Cobbs
Project Editor: Lacie Pinyan
Design Director: Melissa Clark
Photo Director: Paden Reich
Photographers: Antonis Achilleos, Caitlin Bensel,
Jennifer Causey, Greg DuPree, David McClister,
Alison Miksch, Victor Protasio, Jason Wallis
Prop Stylists: Cindy Barr, Mary Clayton Carl,
Kay E. Clarke, Audrey Davis, Taylor Colson Horton,
Claire Spollen
Food Stylists: Mary Claire Britton, Torie Cox,
Margaret Monroe Dickey, Emily Nabors Hall,
Anna Hampton, Tami Hardeman, Tina Stamos
Senior Production Manager: Greg A. Amason
Copy Editors: Donna Baldone, Dolores Hydock
Proofreader: Rebecca Brennan
Indexer: Mary Ann Laurens
Fellows: Holly Ravazzolo, Hanna Yokeley

ISBN-13: 978-0-8487-5763-2
Library of Congress Control Number: 2018949749
First Edition 2018
Printed in the United States of America
10 9 8 7 6 5 4 3 2 1

We welcome your comments and suggestions
about Time Inc. Books.
Time Inc. Books
Attention: Book Editors
P.O. Box 62310
Tampa, Florida 33662-2310

Time Inc. Books products may be purchased for
business or promotional use.

For information on bulk purchases, please contact
Christi Crowley in the Special Sales Department at
(845) 895-9858.

CONTENTS

INTRODUCTION

I've been singing since I can remember and making records since 1992. I love it! It's been a huge part of my life and who I am and I don't want to stop doing it anytime soon. But I also have a passion for cooking for my family and friends. After such a long career in music, the fact that I am now writing a second cookbook really blows me away. I'm so grateful to have another opportunity to share some of my favorite recipes with you.

Over the years, I've noticed how much cooking and singing have in common. When I make something delicious, I want to share it, which is a lot like sharing my music with an audience. I often say that cooking is my love language. I enjoy it because I've seen how it makes the ones I love happy and content. In return, it makes me feel like I've taken good care of them. It's the same way I feel when I walk offstage after a performance.

This book is called *Martina's Kitchen Mix—My Recipe Playlist for Real Life* because it takes you inside my kitchen and shows you what I'm cooking right now. My cooking, like my music, is always evolving. I still have so much to learn! Honestly, I'm finally to the point as a cook where I'm comfortable making up recipes on my own, tweaking recipes I find that I want to try, or fixing a recipe that didn't work the first time. It takes lots of practice and not being afraid to experiment or make mistakes, but the more I cook, read about food, and try new things, the easier it is to be creative.

When I experience new flavors or ways to use herbs, spices, or other ingredients, I start imagining all the different ways I might incorporate them into my cooking. It's a lot like making records where, as you go along, you learn about different instruments. Until you know what each one sounds like, there's no way to imagine how to use them to enhance your music. I had been making records for about seven years the first time my producer mentioned using a *bouzouki* on a song we were tracking in the studio. It's a Greek stringed instrument that has a really cool sound—a little like a mix between a Dobro and a mandolin. At the time, I'd never heard of it, so had no idea how it sounded. Once I did, its sound was in my repertoire and I ended up using it on several records. An ingredient is a lot like that bouzouki in my mind. Until you're familiar with it, it's impossible to imagine how to use it or what it might add to a dish. After you've tasted it, you start imagining all the ways it can liven up and personalize your cooking.

I don't think I'll ever stop learning, nor do I want to. As health and nutrition continue to be important topics of conversation, it seems like new ingredient options are in the spotlight every day—almond milk, cashew butter, nutritional yeast. My oldest daughter often shows me how to incorporate these healthier alternatives into my cooking. (If you know and use them, feel free to apply them to the recipes in this book.) Today, we have Google and YouTube and so many powerful resources at our fingertips, and I learn so much by researching, watching videos, and reading cookbooks by amazing cooks around the world. I'm always trying for balance in life. I believe in moderation, not deprivation, when it comes to food, but I also agree with the old saying, "You are what you eat," and believe that high-quality, nutritious food is imperative for good health. In other words, I try to eat healthy 90% of the time, but sometimes I just want cheese or something else creamy and comforting. So when those cravings hit me, I pay attention, and try and satisfy them. Usually, allowing myself just a little bit of whatever it is I'm craving does the trick and then I don't overdo it.

Recently, I was looking through my old journals and it surprised me just how much my ideas about food have changed. My travels as a performer have exposed me to a variety of foods and that has influenced the way that I cook. The focus on organic foods and healthy diets has changed the way we cook and eat at home. As a matter of fact, we have basically cut out fast food and processed ingredients in our house. After eating mostly fresh, nonprocessed food for a few years now, my taste buds have changed and I find that fast food just doesn't taste as good to me as it once did (ok . . . with the exception of In-N-Out Burger . . . that always tastes good!).

My grandma had this in her kitchen and from about the age of 6 or 7,
I would read from it, as our prayer, before each meal. When I moved away
she gave it to me and it's been in every one of my kitchens since.

When I was growing up on a farm in Kansas, nutrition hadn't become the cultural phenomenon it is today. I had never seen any bread other than Wonder white bread (we ate it slathered with margarine at every meal), and our dinners (or suppers, in Kansas farmspeak) consisted of mostly meat and potatoes. We had a big garden and always had fresh tomatoes and vegetables in the summer (literally farm-to-table), but we didn't have a big supermarket within a 90-mile radius, so when fresh vegetables were out of season, they just weren't available like they are now. Therefore, we ate mostly commercially canned fruits and vegetables. Having access to fresh organic produce year-round is a big advantage, health-wise.

When I'm cooking, my imagination lets loose and rarely do I stick to a recipe as written—if I'm using a recipe at all. I've become an intuitive cook who knows what a dish needs to suit my tastes. It was important to me to create recipes for this book that were versatile enough for you to do the same. I even include "ad-lib" tips to give you ideas for inspired riffs you might consider. It's meant to encourage you to start thinking about cooking "outside the lines" and to be unafraid to experiment or tweak a recipe to your liking. That's what I've been going for in my own kitchen. It's what makes cooking fun!

I've included several family favorites and memories from my childhood with the "Don't Knock It 'Til You Try It" recipes. Every family has quirky or special recipes that have been handed down. I wanted to share some of mine with you.

I hope you enjoy this book and cook from it often. It's my biggest wish that a few of these dishes will make it onto your list of new favorites. Thanks for reading and for following along on my culinary journey.

Love,

Martina

CAST OF CHARACTERS

I talk a lot about my family in this book. I'm proud to have raised three girls who love healthy food and love to eat! Fans of my music most likely know about my family because, well, with social media, how could they not? For those of you who have picked up this book because you heard about it from a friend or the cover caught your eye, let me introduce you to my family.

John: Husband of 30 years. We met in Wichita, Kansas, when I was trying to put a band together to go on the road and he had a rehearsal space for rent. I was a local singer and he owned a local sound company. We have been a team ever since. He has benefitted from my growing knowledge and passion for healthy food over the past few years. This man had never had a tomato when I met him. Or iced tea. Or asparagus, eggplant, or fish in any way, shape, or form (not even fish sticks!). We called him the "food virgin." Now he eats all kinds of things he never would have imagined himself eating and he enjoys it! He's also the best dad and partner (and sound engineer) I could have ever asked for.

Delaney: Daughter #1. She came into our world after 6½ years of marriage and brought sunshine and a deeper glow into our already colorful world. She is now a young adult, 23 at the time of this writing, and really great in the kitchen. She is a personal chef for a company here in Nashville and has taught me so much about modern cooking and all the lifestyle plans like Whole 30 and Paleo. She has a teeny, tiny kitchen in a house she rents with 3 friends and so she cooks at my house for her clients several times a week. I would be lying if I said I didn't love every second she is here in my kitchen.

Emma: Daughter #2. Came along 3½ years after Delaney and there's never been a dull moment since. She is in LA pursuing her dream of acting and really has very little interest in cooking. She loves eating and enjoys healthy and nutritious food but just isn't that interested in spending her time in the kitchen. But that's ok! We who do like to cook need someone to cook for! I'm very impressed with her, living all by herself in such a huge city and going after her dreams at barely 20 years old.

Ava: And here comes Daughter #3. She came along 10 years after Delaney and 7½ after Emma, and our lives were enriched beyond belief. She is 13 and incredibly witty, smart, funny, and complex (in the best way). She is a very independent cook and usually cooks when I'm not in the room and has never once asked for my help. But she makes the best scrambled eggs I've ever tasted.

MARTINA'S KITCHEN MIX

BREAKFAST & BRUNCH

THOUGH IT'S BEEN TOUTED AS THE MOST IMPORTANT MEAL OF THE DAY, I will admit that I don't eat breakfast every day. Sometimes it's all I can do to get myself out the door in the morning, let alone make a big breakfast. That's why I've included recipes in this chapter that can be made a day ahead and eaten throughout the week. If you're in a hurry, just zip up some Cherry-Orange-Almond Granola (page 16) in a bag along with some fresh blueberries for eating in your car. It doesn't even need milk!

While I don't usually get too excited about breakfast, brunch is a different story. I love the idea of mixing and matching breakfast and lunch dishes to make a meal that is unique and can be different each and every time. Also, there's something that always feels a little decadent (in a good way) about brunch. Maybe it's the mimosas (Champagne in the morning? Hello!), or maybe it's the relaxed pace and knowing you can take your time and soak up the day without having to rush. Whatever it is, I love it.

One of my favorite things in life is to sit around a table with friends or family on a lazy weekend morning for a delicious brunch. Nashville has recently exploded with restaurant options. It seems everyone is brunching these days! While it's fun to go to a restaurant, there's something special about having friends over to your house, making a few tasty dishes, serving up coffee and mimosas—like my Sparkling Grapefruit Mimosas (page 57)—and taking time to really catch up with each other. My favorite brunches are the ones that stretch on into a long, laid-back afternoon. When no one is in a hurry, it's a perfect time to relax, laugh, put on some music, and enjoy each other's company.

So start planning a brunch! Most of the recipes you will find in this chapter may be made ahead, but if you're really pressed for time or it's been a crazy-busy week, ask your friends to bring something and make it a potluck brunch. Better yet, assign each of them a recipe from this chapter. Do whatever it takes to make it happen. You won't be sorry, I promise.

Cherry-Orange-Almond Granola

This is so easy to make and easily lasts for two weeks in an airtight container. I love to use it as a topping for plain yogurt as it's a little on the sweet side. If you like your granola less sweet, or you are going to use it with milk or almond milk, simply cut back a bit on the brown sugar.

SERVES 12   HANDS-ON 25 MINUTES   TOTAL 55 MINUTES

½ cup canola oil

1 cup packed brown sugar

¼ cup honey

4 cups uncooked old-fashioned oats

½ cup slivered almonds

½ cup plain sunflower seeds

¼ cup wheat germ

¼ cup ground flax seeds

1 tablespoon orange zest

1 teaspoon vanilla extract

½ cup dried cherries

1. Preheat the oven to 300°F.

2. Heat the oil, brown sugar, and honey in a small saucepan over medium just until warmed through, about 5 minutes.

3. Stir together the oats, almonds, sunflower seeds, wheat germ, flax seeds, orange zest, and vanilla in a large bowl. Stir in the warmed sugar mixture, tossing to coat. Transfer to a lightly greased large rimmed baking sheet.

4. Bake for 30 to 40 minutes, stirring occasionally, or until golden brown. Let cool completely; stir in the dried cherries. Store in an airtight container for up to 2 weeks.

AD LIB

This basic granola is great to experiment with to find your favorite blend. Add flaked coconut or chocolate chips. It would be amazing with the addition of toasted pecans or walnuts. Substitute dried cranberries for the cherries if you like those better.

Avocado Toast with Corn-and-Tomato Salsa

I first made this for an Easter brunch for my family, and the consensus was that it tastes like summer on grilled bread. All these fresh, ripe flavors come together to make one delicious toast. If you don't have a grill or a grill pan, toast in a 350°F oven for 5 to 7 minutes, flipping halfway through, and then brush the bread with olive oil. (Or just stick it in the toaster!) You really can't go wrong with this topping.

SERVES 6   HANDS-ON 30 MINUTES   TOTAL 30 MINUTES

1. Preheat a grill to medium-high (about 400°F).

2. Grill the corn, covered, 20 minutes or until charred, turning every 4 to 5 minutes. Let cool and cut the kernels from the cobs. Discard the cobs.

3. Combine the tomatoes, green onions, jalapeño, corn, and lime juice in a medium bowl.

4. Season to taste with salt. Scoop the avocado into a small bowl and gently mash, using a fork. Spread the avocado mash evenly onto each toast. Top evenly with the corn and tomato mixture. Serve immediately.

> **TIP:** Taking the seeds and veins out of the jalapeño before chopping makes it less spicy. Leave them in if you want a spicier version.

2 ears of corn (about 1 cup corn kernels)

3 plum tomatoes, diced (1 cup diced tomatoes)

2 green onions, thinly sliced (about ¼ cup)

1 jalapeño, finely chopped

1 tablespoon lime juice (from 1 lime)

3 ripe avocados, cut in half and pitted

6 slices crusty white bread, such as sourdough or ciabatta, toasted or grilled

AD LIB

You can also serve this delicious salsa with chips or as a topping for grilled chicken. If you want a little extra spice, sprinkle crushed red pepper on top. Feel free to boil the corn instead of grilling.

Springtime (or Anytime) Quiche

This is based on one of my favorite recipes, Zucchini, Sun-Dried Tomato, and Basil Tart, from my first book. I switched out the zucchini for asparagus and added ham, giving it a classic flavor combination. The herbs, soy sauce, and Dijon take it over the top. I like to serve this with a fresh green salad and sliced ripe tomatoes for brunch or dinner.

SERVES 6   HANDS-ON 30 MINUTES   TOTAL 1 HOUR, 25 MINUTES

½ (14.1-ounce) package refrigerated piecrust

2 teaspoons olive oil

¼ pound asparagus, trimmed and cut into pieces

3 green onions, chopped (about ¼ cup)

1 cup chopped cooked ham

1 garlic clove, minced

2 large eggs

1 large egg white

1 cup half-and-half (or whole milk)

1 teaspoon soy sauce

2 tablespoons Dijon mustard

¼ teaspoon kosher salt

¼ teaspoon freshly ground black pepper

1½ cups grated Swiss cheese

½ cup plus 2 tablespoons grated Parmesan cheese

1 tablespoon chopped fresh oregano

1 tablespoon chopped fresh basil

1. Preheat the oven to 425°F.

2. Fit piecrust into a 9-inch deep-dish pie plate according to package directions; fold edges under, and crimp. Prick bottom and sides of piecrust with a fork.

3. Line pastry with aluminum foil, and fill with pie weights or dried beans. Bake for 7 minutes. Remove the weights and foil, and bake 3 to 4 more minutes or until bottom is golden brown. Reduce oven temperature to 400°F.

4. While piecrust is cooking, heat oil in a medium skillet over medium-high. Add asparagus and green onions, and cook 5 minutes, stirring occasionally, or just until asparagus is tender. Stir in ham and garlic and cook 1 minute longer. Let cool slightly.

5. Whisk together eggs, egg white, half-and-half, soy sauce, Dijon mustard, salt, and pepper in a medium bowl.

6. Sprinkle Swiss cheese over bottom of pastry shell. Top with ½ cup of the Parmesan cheese, oregano, basil, and the ham and asparagus mixture. Pour the egg mixture over top. Sprinkle with the remaining 2 tablespoons Parmesan cheese.

7. Bake for 35 to 40 minutes or until a knife inserted in the center comes out clean, shielding crust with aluminum foil, if necessary. Transfer to a wire rack and let cool for 10 minutes before serving.

TIP: If your quiche isn't quite done but you're in a pinch to get it on the table, just stick it in the microwave for 60 seconds. This will help the eggs set up.

AD LIB

You could try this with roasted garlic instead of fresh. It will add a great depth to the dish. You might also try this with ½ cup cooked, chopped bacon instead of ham (or leave out the meat altogether for a vegetarian version). Substitute other veggies for the asparagus too. I like cauliflower, broccoli, or zucchini, and have been known to add a few drained and chopped sun-dried tomatoes to the mix for a flavorful, colorful boost.

Menu

CLASSIC PARISIAN
Jambon, butter, gherkins   MINI SAVORY PICKLES

PARIS DELUXE
FRENCH HAM → Jambon, butter, brie

LYONNAIS
SALAMI, butter, gherkins

FRENCH COUNTRY
COUNTRY STYLE PORK PATE → French pate, Dijon, gherkins

PROVENCE
Grilled veggies, hummus, herb de provence

DRINKS

Savory Tarts

Cheddar Biscuits with Bacon

These savory and flavorful biscuits are so easy and versatile. They would be delicious broken up and sprinkled in a soup in place of crackers or made into an egg and cheese sandwich for a quick and hearty breakfast treat. Slather them with your favorite sweet jam or jelly or enjoy them all by themselves. The original recipe didn't call for bacon. (That was my idea. You're welcome!) So if bacon is not your thing, just leave it out. You could also try adding green onions or chives to the batter.

SERVES 6   HANDS-ON 30 MINUTES   TOTAL 45 MINUTES

1. Preheat the oven to 450°F.

2. Line a baking sheet with parchment paper or lightly coat with vegetable oil.

3. Whisk together the flour, sugar, baking powder, and salt in a large bowl. Cut in the butter with a pastry blender, or use 2 knives, until the butter is the size of peas; stir in the cheese and bacon.

4. Combine the buttermilk and egg in a small bowl. Add to the flour mixture just until incorporated. Turn the dough out onto a lightly floured surface, and pat or roll the dough to ³/₄-inch thickness; cut with a 3-inch round cutter, and place on the prepared baking sheet.

5. Bake for 12 to 14 minutes or until golden brown.

TIP. If you're in a rush, these work great as drop biscuits. Using an ice cream scoop or ¹/₄-cup measuring cup, drop the batter onto the prepared pan.

2½ cups all-purpose flour

¹/₄ cup sugar

1 tablespoon baking powder

1 teaspoon kosher salt

6 tablespoons unsalted cold butter, cubed

1 cup shredded sharp Cheddar cheese

6 pieces smoked bacon, cooked and chopped

1 cup buttermilk

1 large egg, beaten

Hash Brown Breakfast Casserole with Tomato Gravy

A few years ago I decided it would be great to start the tradition of sitting down to a big family breakfast on Christmas morning. With all the other cooking I do that day, I wanted to find a breakfast casserole recipe that I could prepare the night before and pop into the oven while we finished opening presents. This is a hearty casserole with all the breakfast flavor favorites—potatoes, cheese, eggs, and sausage. But what really makes this casserole stand out is the tomato gravy. I serve it in a bowl or pitcher at the table and just let everyone top their own serving. It's so delicious and great on biscuits too!

SERVES 8   HANDS-ON 35 MINUTES   TOTAL 1 HOUR

1 (32-ounce) bag frozen diced or shredded hash brown potatoes

1 (8-ounce) block sharp Cheddar cheese, grated (about 2 cups)

1 small sweet onion, chopped (about ½ cup)

1 teaspoon kosher salt

½ teaspoon black pepper

3 large eggs, beaten

1 (16-ounce) container sour cream

1 (16-ounce) package ground pork sausage, roughly chopped

3 tablespoons all-purpose flour

2 (14.5-ounce) cans petite diced tomatoes, undrained

½ cup heavy cream

Garnish: chopped fresh chives

1. Preheat the oven to 350°F.

2. Stir together the hash browns, 1½ cups of the cheese, and the onion, salt, pepper, eggs, and sour cream.

3. Cook the sausage in a large skillet 10 minutes or until lightly browned. Remove from the skillet with a slotted spoon, reserving the drippings in the pan. Add the flour to the pan, and cook for 1 minute, stirring constantly. Add the tomatoes with juice, and cook 5 minutes or until thickened. Reduce the heat to low, and stir in the cream. Season to taste with salt and pepper. Set aside, keeping warm.

4. In a large bowl, stir the sausage into the hash brown mixture, and transfer to a lightly greased 13- x 9-inch baking dish. Top with the remaining ½ cup cheese. Bake until just set and golden brown, 30 minutes.

5. Spoon the casserole onto serving plates; top with the warm tomato gravy and a sprinkling of chives, if desired.

Quick Rice with Milk, Cinnamon, and Sugar

—

We weren't really a "big breakfast" kind of family growing up, but I do remember my mom making this for us before school. Interestingly, I never made it for my girls, but my sister brought it up during one of our recent conversations about food and childhood (along with the canned tamales we used to eat that came wrapped in paper . . . anyone remember those???). The warm rice with the cold milk and a dash of cinnamon is so comforting.

SERVES 4   HANDS-ON 10 MINUTES   TOTAL 10 MINUTES

1. Bring the water to a boil in a small saucepan. Add the rice; remove from the heat, and cover. Let stand 5 minutes or until the water is absorbed. Stir in the butter.

2. Stir together the sugar and cinnamon. Transfer the rice to serving bowls, and sprinkle evenly with the sugar and cinnamon. Divide the cold milk over the rice, and sprinkle with ground cinnamon, if desired. Serve immediately.

2 cups water

2 cups uncooked quick cooking rice (such as Minute Rice)

2 tablespoons butter

3 tablespoons sugar

½ teaspoon ground cinnamon

1 cup cold milk

Garnish: ground cinnamon

AD LIB

You could make a whole-grain, dairy-free version with brown rice (adjust cooking time accordingly) and almond milk.

DON'T KNOCK IT 'TIL YOU TRY IT

My dad made this favorite from my childhood for us every now and then. We considered it a real treat and had it alongside eggs, or sometimes all by itself. It was something passed down from his parents and maybe even before them. (A version of it is on the side of the Quaker Yellow Corn Meal box.) I make it only occasionally for obvious waistline reasons, but it's soooo delicious— crispy on the outside, warm and soft on the inside. Mmmm!

Fried Cornmeal "Mush"

SERVES 4   HANDS-ON 30 MINUTES
TOTAL 8 HOURS, 30 MINUTES, INCLUDING 8 HOURS CHILLING

4 cups water

1 cup plain white cornmeal

1 teaspoon kosher salt

⅓ cup vegetable oil

Butter, jelly, or honey, to serve

1. Bring 3 cups of the water to a boil in a 3½-quart saucepan. Whisk together the remaining 1 cup water, cornmeal, and salt in a medium bowl. Pour the cornmeal mixture into the boiling water, whisking constantly. Cook over medium until thickened, stirring frequently, about 5 minutes. Cover and cook on low until very thick and bubbly, about 5 minutes.

2. Pour the mixture into a buttered 9- x 5-inch loaf pan. Let cool completely. Cover with plastic wrap, and refrigerate 8 hours or overnight.

3. Turn out onto a cutting board, and slice into 1-inch slices. Heat the oil in a large nonstick skillet over medium-high. Cook the slices, 3 minutes on each side, or until golden brown.

4. Serve warm with butter, jelly, or honey, or eat plain.

FRIED MUSH
TO MAKE FRIED MUSH - 4 CUPS Water 4 tsp
SALT - BRING 3 CUPS WATER TO A BOIL
THEN ADD 1 CUP water by wisking in - STIR
WHITE CORN MEAL COVER & SIMMER FOR 5
UNTIL THICKENED. COVER & SIMMER FOR 5
MIN - REMOVE & PUT INTO A LOAF PAN
PUT IN REF OVER NIGHT - MORNING REMOVE
& TAKE OUT OF PAN AND SLICE INTO 4"
SLICES - PLACE SLICES IN SKILLET 4.
VEG. OIL - FRY UNTIL ALMOST LR.
REMOVE - BUTTER SLICES & EAT W/
EGGS OR BY ITSELF -

Baked French Toast with Pecan Crumble and Blackberry-Maple Syrup

This is a decadent dish that is perfect for brunch with friends or family. I always get requests for this recipe. You can make the crumble and syrup a day ahead. Just store the pecan crumble mixture in an airtight container and the Blackberry-Maple Syrup in the fridge. In the morning, top with the crumble and then just pop the baking dish in the oven, and you will soon have people following their noses to the kitchen!

**SERVES 8 TO 10 HANDS-ON 40 MINUTES
TOTAL 11 HOURS, 40 MINUTES, INCLUDING SYRUP**

1 (16-ounce) loaf challah, sliced
  1 inch thick
4 large eggs
4 large egg yolks
2 cups heavy cream
2 cups whole milk
¼ cup sugar
1 teaspoon vanilla extract
½ teaspoon ground cinnamon
½ teaspoon ground nutmeg
¾ teaspoon kosher salt
½ cup pecan halves
2 tablespoons chilled unsalted
  butter, cut into pieces
2 tablespoons light brown sugar
Blackberry-Maple Syrup
  (recipe follows)
Garnish: powdered sugar

1. Spread out the bread on a rimmed baking sheet. Cover with a clean kitchen towel, and let stand overnight.

2. Butter a 13- x 9-inch baking dish. Arrange the bread slices, overlapping, in rows in the prepared dish.

3. Whisk together the eggs, egg yolks, cream, milk, sugar, vanilla, cinnamon, nutmeg, and ½ teaspoon of the salt in a medium bowl. Pour over the bread, pressing the bread to help it soak in the liquid. Cover and chill at least 2 hours or overnight.

4. Preheat the oven to 350°F.

5. Pulse the pecans, butter, brown sugar, and remaining ¼ teaspoon salt in a food processor until the nuts are coarsely chopped, about 5 or 6 times.

6. Scatter the pecan crumble over the soaked bread, and cover the baking dish tightly with foil. Bake for 25 to 30 minutes or until warmed through. Remove the foil, and bake until deeply browned and puffed up, 35 to 40 minutes. Serve with the Blackberry-Maple Syrup, and a sprinkling of powdered sugar, if desired.

TIP: The bread needs to be "day-old" bread so you may want to let it sit out. Soak the dry slices for at least 2 hours or overnight before baking.

Blackberry-Maple Syrup

1 (12-ounce) bag frozen blackberries,
  thawed (or 12 ounces fresh blackberries)

3 tablespoons lemon juice
  (from 1 large lemon)

2 tablespoons sugar

1 cup pure maple syrup

Stir together the blackberries, lemon juice, and sugar in a 3½-quart saucepan.
Bring to a boil; reduce the heat, stirring occasionally, 10 minutes or just until the
berries soften and slightly thicken. Remove from the heat, and stir in the maple syrup.
Serve warm. Makes 2½ cups

Grandma's Cinnamon Rolls

My grandma was one of the first people, other than my mom, I spent a lot of time with in the kitchen. She was such a great cook and it seemed like she was always making something delicious. Every once in awhile she would make these cinnamon rolls and her house would smell like heaven.

**SERVES 16   HANDS-ON 40 MINUTES
TOTAL 2 HOURS, 40 MINUTES, INCLUDING GLAZE**

1 (¼-ounce) package active
   dry yeast
½ teaspoon plus ¼ cup sugar
½ cup warm water (100° to
   110°F)
1 cup milk at room temperature
¼ cup shortening (such as
   Crisco)
½ teaspoon kosher salt
4 cups all-purpose flour
½ cup softened butter
¾ cup packed brown sugar
2 tablespoons ground
   cinnamon
Vanilla Glaze (recipe follows)

1. Combine the yeast, ½ teaspoon of the sugar, and warm water in a mixer fitted with the dough attachment; let stand 5 minutes or until bubbly.

2. Stir together the remaining ¼ cup sugar, milk, shortening, and salt. Add to the yeast mixture, beating at medium speed until combined. Beat in the flour at medium-low speed, 1 cup at a time, until a soft dough forms.

3. Turn the dough out onto a well-floured surface, and knead until smooth and elastic (about 2 minutes). Place in a well-greased bowl, turning to grease the top. Cover the dough with plastic wrap, and let rise in a warm (80° to 85°F) place, free from drafts, 1 to 2 hours or until doubled in size.

4. Punch the dough down. Turn the dough out onto a lightly floured surface, and roll into a 16- x 12-inch rectangle (about ¼ inch thick). Spread with the softened butter, leaving a 1-inch border around the edges.

5. Stir together the brown sugar and cinnamon; sprinkle evenly over the top. Roll up the dough jelly-roll fashion, starting at 1 long end. Cut into 16 (1-inch-thick) slices, using a serrated knife. Transfer the slices, cut sides down, to a lightly greased 13- x 9-inch baking dish. Cover and let rise in a warm (80° to 85°F) place, free from drafts, 30 to 45 minutes or until doubled in size.

6. Preheat the oven to 350°F.

7. Bake for 20 to 25 minutes or until golden brown. Drizzle the glaze over the warm rolls.

Vanilla Glaze

4 tablespoons butter, melted

4 tablespoons milk

2 cups powdered sugar

1 teaspoon vanilla extract

Whisk together the butter, milk, powdered sugar, and vanilla in a medium bowl.
Makes about 1 cup

MARTINA'S KITCHEN MIX

COCKTAILS & APPETIZERS

COCKTAILS AND APPETIZERS are quite possibly my favorite part of a meal or dinner party. They can really set the mood for the evening. Beer and wine are easy and they always work, but there's something about making and sharing a cocktail that's a little more festive and special. Recently, we took a family trip to Italy. I quickly became familiar with the term "aperitivo," which means "appetizer" or "light meal." Friends gather at a bar or in the living room before dinner for small bites and a predinner cocktail or soda. Simple, savory bites like potato chips, peanuts, or even popcorn are served. It's so laid-back and fun! It's their version of the American "happy hour" or "cocktail hour."

Cocktail hour at home is not as common now as it was in the fifties, so it seems special and a little luxurious. I say we bring it back! It's such a good transition from the hustle and bustle of the day and lets you ease into the evening to come. Having a cocktail or mocktail and a couple of tasty bites ready when your guests arrive is a treat and, as I say, quite civilized. For appetizers, I love small bites that can be popped into your mouth while holding a drink (no fork and knife required). In this chapter, I've grouped cocktails with appetizers that complement one another to take away the guesswork.

As much as I would love to learn more about craft cocktails, if there's a cocktail recipe with spirits or ingredients I've never heard of, I'll most likely skip it. (Maybe I'll take up mixology on my next break from touring. It's either that, learn Italian, or learn to throw pottery. Hmmmmm . . . maybe I'll do all three!) If you're looking for fancy-schmancy cocktails or you are a legit bartender, this chapter might be too basic for you, but if you want easy, tasty drinks that can be made spur of the moment with ingredients you already have on hand, then I've got whatcha came for.

While in Italy, I discovered the Negroni. Made with equal parts gin (I prefer Hendrick's), sweet vermouth, and Campari, it's a bittersweet aperitif that whets your appetite for the meal to come. It was exciting and kind of romantic to be sipping a drink in the country where it was invented, and I knew I had to put the recipe in this book so you could taste it as well. I still love the "Martina Margarita" from my first book, so I've created a twist on it with my Grapefruit Margaritas (page 58). Grapefruit is my new jam when it comes to cocktails so I've included not one but three cocktails with a grapefruit theme. The refreshing Blackberry-Lemon Gin and Tonic (page 40) is another great drink—perfect for summer evenings on the patio. If curling up after dinner with a rich, whiskey-laced Irish Coffee is more your speed, you can find the definitive version right here (page 86). Cheers!

Blackberry-Lemon Gin and Tonic

This cocktail is a delight for the senses. Crisp and colorful, this refresher is perfect to serve guests as a predinner cocktail in spring or summer. Muddling the mint and blackberries is an important step because it releases the juices from both and makes for a more interesting flavor. If you don't have a muddler, put it on your birthday list. Until then, use the back of a long-handled spoon to get the job done.

SERVES 2   HANDS-ON 5 MINUTES   TOTAL 5 MINUTES

6 blackberries

10 mint leaves

Juice from 1 lemon

2 tablespoons Simple Syrup (recipe follows)

6 ounces good-quality gin (I prefer Hendrick's)

Tonic water

Garnishes: lemon slices, blackberries, mint sprigs

1. Combine and muddle the blackberries, mint leaves, lemon juice, and Simple Syrup in a cocktail shaker until the berries and mint are crushed. Add the gin, and shake well.

2. Fill 2 glasses with ice. Strain the mixture over ice. Top with tonic water, and garnish with a slice of lemon, a blackberry, and a mint sprig, if desired.

Simple Syrup

Combine 1 cup sugar and 1 cup water in a small saucepan. Cook over medium, stirring occasionally, just until the sugar dissolves, about 5 to 6 minutes. Remove from the heat, and let cool completely. Makes about 1 cup

 Simple Syrup can be stored in the refrigerator for up to 1 week.

AD LIB

Try this same recipe, replacing the gin with bourbon, for a Blackberry Julep.

Whipped Feta Crostini with Roasted Garlic, Tomatoes, and Herbs

I gotta be honest, when it comes to hors d'oeuvres (that fancy French word for appetizers), I think it's hard to beat toasted bread with yummy toppings. Crostini is always a crowd-pleaser. It's pretty, easy to eat in one or two bites, and delicious. The whipped feta is creamy and tangy. (Add a bit more cream cheese to tame that tanginess if you'd like.) Roasted garlic adds a nice depth of flavor. I've included two favorite variations for you to try!

SERVES 6 TO 8   HANDS-ON 30 MINUTES   TOTAL 1 HOUR, 5 MINUTES

1 large garlic bulb

1 tablespoon plus 2 teaspoons extra-virgin olive oil

1/2 teaspoon kosher salt

1/8 teaspoon smoked paprika

2 pints grape tomatoes, halved

1 (16-ounce) loaf ciabatta bread, sliced into 1/2-inch-thick slices

1 (8-ounce) package feta cheese, at room temperature

1 cup whipped cream cheese, at room temperature, or more to taste

1 tablespoon chopped fresh rosemary

2 teaspoons chopped fresh thyme

Extra-virgin olive oil, for drizzling (optional)

1. Preheat the oven to 425°F.

2. Cut off the pointed end of the garlic bulb; place the entire unpeeled bulb of garlic on a piece of aluminum foil, and drizzle with 2 teaspoons of the olive oil. Sprinkle with 1/2 teaspoon of the salt and the paprika. Fold the foil to seal the packet. Toss the grape tomatoes with the remaining 1 tablespoon olive oil on a rimmed baking sheet. Add the foil packet of garlic to 1 side of the baking sheet. Roast for 15 minutes, and then remove the tomatoes from the baking sheet; set aside. Roast the garlic 20 minutes more. Remove the garlic from the oven. Carefully open the foil, and let cool 20 minutes. When cool enough to handle, squeeze the pulp from the papery skins with your fingers.

3. While the garlic is cooling, place the bread slices on the rimmed baking sheet in the oven. Toast the bread until lightly browned, 5 to 7 minutes, turning the slices halfway through to toast evenly.

4. While the bread is toasting, process the feta cheese and cream cheese in a food processor for 3 minutes or until smooth, scraping down the sides as necessary. Taste and add more cream cheese, a tablespoon at a time, if you want it to be a little sweeter.

5. To assemble, spread 1 side of the toasted bread slices with the roasted garlic pulp, and top with a layer of the feta spread. Spread the roasted tomatoes evenly on top of each slice, and sprinkle with the chopped herbs. Drizzle with extra-virgin olive oil, if desired.

variations

To serve 6 to 8, use 1 (16-ounce) loaf ciabatta bread, sliced into ½-inch-thick slices for each of these variations.

Grilled Peach and Pancetta: whipped feta spread (see Step 4 at left) • 2 peaches, peeled and sliced • 6 thin slices pancetta • ½ cup chopped walnuts, lightly toasted (see page 106) • 2 cups loosely packed baby arugula • 3 tablespoons honey. Heat a cast-iron grill pan over high. Coat the pan with cooking spray. Cook the peach slices for 3 minutes per side or just until lightly charred. Cook the pancetta in a medium skillet 2 to 3 minutes per side over medium or until just crisp. Top the crostini with the feta spread, peaches, pancetta, chopped toasted walnuts, and arugula, and drizzle with honey.

Warm Date and Balsamic: whipped feta spread (see Step 4 at left) • 4 slices bacon • ½ cup chopped dates • ½ cup crumbled smoked blue cheese • 3 tablespoons balsamic glaze • 1 tablespoon minced fresh rosemary (optional). Cook the bacon in a large skillet over medium-high 8 to 10 minutes or until crisp; remove the bacon to drain on paper towels, reserving 1 tablespoon drippings in the skillet. When cool, crumble the bacon. Add the chopped dates to the skillet, and cook over medium 3 to 4 minutes, stirring occasionally, or just until warmed through. Top the crostini with the feta spread, crumbled bacon, warm dates, and blue cheese. Drizzle with the balsamic glaze, and garnish with a pinch of minced fresh rosemary, if desired.

AD LIB

I just love roasted garlic, but honestly this is equally delicious without the garlic. Just leave out the roasting step to save some time. You will still get rave reviews. Of course, the variations provide a few other riffs on the theme that are worth trying.

Grilled Sweet Peppers with Goat Cheese and Herbs

I saw bags of these cute little red, yellow, and orange sweet peppers in the grocery store one day and I wondered what I could do with them. They are so colorful, and I just immediately thought "appetizer!" This is an easy, basic recipe I created along with a few variations so you never get bored.

SERVES 8   HANDS-ON 30 MINUTES   TOTAL 30 MINUTES

1. Preheat a grill pan or grill to medium-high (about 450°F).

2. Cut the stems off the peppers, and slice in half lengthwise; remove and discard the seeds and membranes. Place in a large bowl, and drizzle with the olive oil. Toss with the salt, pepper, and smoked paprika.

3. Grill the peppers, uncovered, 2 to 3 minutes, turning often, or just until slightly softened. Spoon the goat cheese evenly into pepper halves. Sprinkle with the rosemary and thyme.

TIP: These are great warm and can be made a day ahead and reheated in a 350°F oven for about 5 minutes. Also, the peppers are easier to fill if the goat cheese is chilled.

1 pound mini sweet peppers
1 tablespoon extra-virgin olive oil
½ teaspoon kosher salt
¼ teaspoon black pepper
¼ teaspoon smoked paprika
1 (4-ounce) package goat cheese
¾ teaspoon finely chopped fresh rosemary
½ teaspoon finely chopped fresh thyme

variations

Goat Cheese and Bacon: Stir 4 slices chopped cooked bacon into the cheese in Step 3. Proceed as directed.

Italian Sausage-Pepper Jack: Prepare as directed, substituting 3 ounces softened cream cheese and ½ cup shredded pepper Jack cheese for the goat cheese in Step 3. Stir in 4 ounces cooked Italian sausage, crumbled, and 2 teaspoons chopped fresh sage. Fill the peppers with the mixture, and sprinkle the batch with about 3 tablespoons panko. Place in a broiler pan, and broil 5 inches from the heat, 1 to 2 minutes or just until golden brown.

Creamy Feta: Prepare as directed, substituting 1 cup of whipped feta spread from Step 4 of the recipe on page 42.

Flavia's Deviled Eggs

I love a good deviled egg recipe. This recipe comes from John's mom. She was an amazing cook and hostess, and I learned so much from her. She cooked for our wedding rehearsal dinner and I cannot figure out how she made Chicken Cordon Bleu for 30 people with a teeny, tiny apartment-size stove. It was like a magic trick! But Flavia was pretty magical. I miss her and am proud to have her recipe in this book.

SERVES 6   HANDS-ON 25 MINUTES   TOTAL 50 MINUTES

6 large eggs
3 tablespoons mayonnaise
1 tablespoon Dijon mustard
½ teaspoon prepared
   horseradish (optional)
1 teaspoon lemon juice
Kosher salt and black pepper
Garnishes: sweet paprika,
   chives, chopped green onions,
   cornichons, cayenne pepper,
   lettuce, radishes

1. Place the eggs in a single layer in a stainless-steel saucepan. (Do not use nonstick.) Add hot water to a depth of 3 inches. Bring to a rolling boil; cover, remove from the heat, and let stand 13 minutes.

2. Drain immediately, and return the eggs to the pan. Fill the pan with cold water and ice. Let eggs cool 10 minutes. Tap each egg firmly on the counter until cracks form all over the shell. Peel under cold running water.

3. Halve the eggs lengthwise while slightly warm; carefully remove the yolks, keeping the egg whites intact. Mash the yolks with the mayonnaise, mustard, horseradish (if desired), lemon juice, and salt and pepper to taste. Spoon the yolk mixture into egg white halves, or use a pastry bag for a more decorative touch. Chill thoroughly.

4. To serve, top with your choice of sweet paprika, chives, chopped green onions, cornichons, or cayenne, if desired. Serve on a platter with lettuce and radishes, if desired.

AD LIB

I love the Dijon mustard in this recipe, but if it's not your thing, you can use regular mustard or start with just a teaspoon of Dijon and add more to suit your taste. If you like your deviled eggs a little sweeter, add a pinch of sugar or a teaspoon of sweet pickle juice. Chopped fresh tarragon added to the mix is good too.

Vodka Limeade Cooler

I love to have people over to my house to hang out. I think it's a great way to make special memories that will last forever. Sometimes a gathering takes a lot of careful planning, but sometimes it's as easy as sending an impromptu group text to "come on over" and then mixing up this simple but delicious three-ingredient cocktail. I like to make this for my girlfriends to sip by the pool with some chips and salsa. It's basically a limeade with vodka and it goes down (dangerously) easy on a hot day. It's pretty served as written, but I also love it in a highball glass (or red Solo cup!) with crushed ice.

SERVES 1   HANDS-ON 5 MINUTES   TOTAL 5 MINUTES

Muddle the lime wedges and Simple Syrup in a cocktail shaker. Add the vodka, and fill with ice. Cover with the lid, and shake vigorously until thoroughly chilled (about 30 seconds). Strain into a chilled martini glass. Garnish with lime slices, if desired. Serve immediately.

1 lime, cut into wedges
1½ teaspoons Simple Syrup (page 40)
2 ounces vodka
Garnish: lime slices

Avocado, Cucumber, and Red Pepper Salsa

Healthy and full of fresh ingredients, this is a lovely variation on the usual salsa. I eat it with tortilla chips but it is also delicious in place of the Cucumber-Tomato Salad suggested with the chicken on page 160.

MAKES 2 CUPS   HANDS-ON 20 MINUTES   TOTAL 40 MINUTES

1 small cucumber, peeled, seeded, and diced (about ½ cup)

1 small red bell pepper, diced (½ cup)

3 green onions, finely chopped (about ¼ cup)

1 jalapeño, seeded and finely chopped

2 teaspoons chopped cilantro

2 tablespoons fresh lime juice

½ teaspoon kosher salt

1 avocado, peeled and diced (1 cup)

Combine the cucumber, red bell pepper, green onions, jalapeño, cilantro, lime juice, and salt in a large bowl. Gently fold in the avocado. Let stand 20 minutes before serving.

AD LIB

Toss this with a little of the Avocado Crema on page 251 to turn it into a side salad. A piece of grilled chicken on top would make it a delicious main course.

John's Spicy Sausage Cheese Dip

The first thing my husband, John, ever cooked for me was a grilled cheese. There was SO much cheese in that sandwich and I figured out that I had found someone who really got me when it came to the whole cheese thing. He doesn't cook often, but he does have a few specialties that I wanted to include in this book. This one isn't going to win any awards for the most health-conscious recipe, but it's absolutely delicious. Every year for the Super Bowl he makes up a big batch of this dip in a slow cooker and serves it with the "scoops" version of corn chips or tortilla chips. We like it spicy but feel free to adjust the Ro-Tel if spicy is not your thing.

SERVES 14   HANDS-ON 20 MINUTES   TOTAL 20 MINUTES

1. Cook the sausage in a skillet over medium, 5 minutes to warm through. Transfer it to a 3-quart slow cooker set to WARM with a slotted spoon.

2. Add the cheese and diced tomatoes and green chiles (with the liquid from the can) to the slow cooker with the sausage, and stir well to combine. Give it a stir from time to time to keep the dip smooth.

AD LIB

Instead of commercial sausage, pick up a favorite smoked sausage from a local BBQ joint (John uses sausage from Jack's BBQ in Nashville). Or, substitute browned crumbled Italian sausage instead.

1 pound smoked sausage, diced

1 (32-ounce) package pasteurized prepared cheese product, cubed (such as Velveeta)

2 (10-ounce) cans diced tomatoes and green chiles, (such as Ro-Tel)

Tortilla chips, for serving

Grapefruit Cocktails Three Ways

I love grapefruit! These are three of my favorite grapefruit cocktails on the next few pages. Grapefruit juice is really refreshing and a nice change of pace from orange juice. (Of course, if you don't like grapefruit juice, any of these cocktails can be made with orange juice.) Two of these contain tequila (you're welcome), and I know I talked about no exotic ingredients, but St-Germain is an elderflower liqueur that is readily available in any liquor store—and it's delicious!

Tequila and Soda with a Grapefruit Splash

SERVES 1   HANDS-ON 5 MINUTES   TOTAL 5 MINUTES

3 ounces blanco tequila
  (such as Patrón Silver)
3 tablespoons freshly
  squeezed grapefruit juice,
  or more to taste
Club soda
Garnish: sliced grapefruit

Stir together the tequila and grapefruit juice in a pint-size serving glass filled with ice. Top with club soda. Garnish, if desired. Serve immediately.

Sparkling Grapefruit Mimosa Cocktails for a Crowd

SERVES 10 TO 12 HANDS-ON 20 MINUTES
TOTAL 2 HOURS, 20 MINUTES, INCLUDING 2 HOURS CHILLING

1. Combine the grapefruit juice, St-Germain, and Campari in a large pitcher. Cover and chill until cold, about 2 hours.

2. If desired, rub the rims of coupe glasses or Champagne flutes with a wedge of grapefruit. Invert each glass in a shallow bowl, just a bit wider than the diameter of the glasses, filled with a thin layer of superfine sugar. Gently twist the glasses to coat the dampened rims in sugar.

3. Divide the chilled grapefruit mixture among coupe glasses or flutes, and top with the chilled Champagne.

2 cups freshly squeezed grapefruit juice (from about 4 grapefruits)

Superfine sugar (optional)

½ cup St-Germain (elderflower liqueur)

¼ cup Campari

1 (750-milliliter) bottle chilled Champagne (or sparkling wine)

Grapefruit Margaritas

SERVES 2   HANDS-ON 20 MINUTES   TOTAL 20 MINUTES

Margarita salt (optional)

¾ cup freshly squeezed Ruby
   Red grapefruit juice (from
   1½ grapefruits)

2 limes, juiced (¼ cup)

3 ounces silver or blanco
   tequila

2 to 3 tablespoons Simple
   Syrup (page 40)

Garnishes: sliced grapefruit,
   lime wedges

1. If desired, rub the rims of 2 margarita or highball glasses with a wedge of grapefruit. Invert each glass in a shallow bowl, just a bit wider than the diameter of the glasses, filled with a thin layer of margarita salt. Gently twist the glasses to coat the dampened rims in salt. Add ice to the glasses.

2. Combine the grapefruit juice, lime juice, tequila, and Simple Syrup in a cocktail shaker filled with ice. Cover with the lid, and shake vigorously until thoroughly chilled (about 30 seconds). Strain into the prepared glasses. Garnish with sliced grapefruit and lime wedges, if desired.

TIP: Ruby Red grapefruit is sweeter than pink grapefruit, so you may need to adjust the amount of Simple Syrup in the drink.

Pitcher-Perfect Grapefruit Margaritas: Stir together 3 cups freshly squeezed grapefruit juice (from about 6 grapefruits), 1 cup lime juice (from about 8 juicy limes), 1½ cups silver or blanco tequila, and ½ to ¾ cup Simple Syrup (page 40) to taste in a large serving pitcher. Cover and chill until ready to serve. Before serving, stir well, and pour into 8 ice-filled, salt-rimmed glasses. Makes about 48 ounces

DON'T KNOCK IT 'TIL YOU TRY IT

John has two "signature dishes" and I've included them both in this book. To be honest, I had never heard of these delicious little bites until we met. He explained that his dad used to make them all the time when they were growing up. Now they are a staple at all of our cookouts, and they're perfect for cocktail hour! I've included a Garlic-Herb version as a bonus recipe.

John's Bacon-Wrapped Olives

SERVES 4   HANDS-ON 30 MINUTES   TOTAL 1 HOUR, 30 MINUTES

25 wooden picks

1 pound smoked bacon (not thick cut), cut into thirds

1 (7-ounce) jar pimiento-stuffed queen olives, drained

1. Soak the wooden picks in water for 1 hour; drain.

2. Preheat a grill to 300° to 350°F (medium).

3. Wrap each piece of bacon around an olive, securing with a wooden pick. Grill over medium, turning often, until the bacon is browned and crisp. Serve warm.

Garlic-Herb Goat Cheese Filling: Mix 2 ounces goat cheese (at room temperature); 2 tablespoons finely grated Parmesan cheese; 1 tablespoon finely chopped fresh herbs such as thyme, chives, or parsley; 1 small garlic clove, finely grated; and 1 teaspoon fresh lemon juice. Use a pastry bag or a resealable plastic bag with the corner cut to stuff large, pitted green olives with this mixture, and then wrap them with the bacon and proceed as directed. Mmmmmm!

AD LIB

Use jalapeño-, garlic-, or blue cheese-stuffed olives. Or stuff olives with the Whipped Feta on page 42.

Smoked Gouda Pimiento Cheese

Ok, get ready for some serious flavor. I absolutely love this! It isn't exactly health food, but when something tastes this good, it's worth the occasional splurge. This is delicious on a sandwich or spread on bread or crackers. I'm just going to warn you . . . it's addictive.

MAKES 4 CUPS   HANDS-ON 20 MINUTES   TOTAL 20 MINUTES

Stir together the mayonnaise, pimientos, Worcestershire, garlic powder, and cayenne in a large bowl; add the cheeses, stirring until blended. Store in the refrigerator up to 1 week.

 Don't skip the step of rinsing your diced pimiento. Otherwise it will be too salty.

AD LIB

Spoon this over hot cooked pasta (rotini or elbow macaroni works great), give it a stir, and broil for a quick and tasty take on mac-and-cheese. Or put it on your baked potato (if I could use emojis in this book, the wide-eyed OMG emoji would be perfect here!).

1 cup mayonnaise

1 (7-ounce) jar diced pimiento, drained and rinsed

1 teaspoon Worcestershire sauce

½ teaspoon garlic powder

¼ to ½ teaspoon cayenne pepper

1 (8-ounce) block extra-sharp Cheddar cheese, shredded (about 2 cups)

1 (8-ounce) block smoked Gouda cheese, shredded (about 2 cups)

Jumby Bay Signature Rum Punch

A few years ago, my family took a bit of a luxury vacation to a place in the Caribbean called Jumby Bay. It's a Rosewood resort and was quite an indulgence! But we had been working really hard on the road and in the studio, and I truly believe in the importance of investing in experiences together that make great memories. There's nothing like traveling together as a family, especially now that our girls are older. I treasure the times we can do that. Anyway . . . oh my goodness . . . they had a drink at the resort simply called Rum Punch. Even all these years later I think about it. So when it came time to write this book, I reached out and asked if they would share the recipe, and they did! Thank you, Jumby Bay, for the great memories and sharing this most delicious cocktail recipe.

SERVES 8   HANDS-ON 10 MINUTES   TOTAL 10 MINUTES

2 cups (16 ounces) orange juice

2 cups (16 ounces) dark rum

½ cup (4 ounces) fresh lime juice

¾ cup (6 ounces) Simple Syrup (page 40)

About 5 teaspoons bitters

Garnishes: fresh pineapple, orange slices

Fill a pitcher one-third full with ice. Add the orange juice, rum, lime juice, Simple Syrup, and bitters. Stir vigorously until chilled (about 30 seconds). Pour into eight 10-ounce cocktail glasses filled with ice. Garnish with pineapple and orange slices, if desired, and serve immediately.

Marinated Goat Cheese with Lemon and Herbs

You may have noticed that I love goat cheese. This is one of my favorite go-to appetizers. With all the red and green, it's beautiful at the holidays, but all the fresh herbs and lemon make it equally fitting for spring and summer as well. It's delicious spread on sliced, toasted (or untoasted) baguette, and I also love it spread on water crackers. The tang and creaminess of goat cheese work so well with the herbs and citrus, and the sun-dried tomatoes add even more flavor to the mix.

SERVES 8   HANDS-ON 25 MINUTES   TOTAL 2 HOURS, 25 MINUTES, INCLUDING 2 HOURS CHILLING

1. Slice the goat cheese into ¼-inch-thick slices, and place in a shallow serving dish with sides. Tuck in the rosemary sprigs. Sprinkle the lemon zest, sun-dried tomatoes, capers, chopped herbs, sea salt, and crushed red pepper, if desired, over the top of the cheese slices and drizzle with the olive oil.

2. Cover and refrigerate at least 2 hours or up to 6 hours to allow the flavors to meld. Remove the platter 15 minutes before serving to allow the cheese to soften.

TIP: Be sure to use good-quality extra-virgin olive oil because it's a big player in this recipe. I like an olive oil that is richly flavored but not bitter. Three of my favorites are Paul Newman's Organic, Frankies 457, and California Olive Ranch.

1 (4-ounce) log goat cheese

3 (3-inch) sprigs fresh rosemary

2 teaspoons lemon zest

2 tablespoons finely chopped, drained oil-packed sun-dried tomatoes

½ teaspoon finely chopped capers

1 teaspoon chopped fresh thyme

1 teaspoon chopped fresh rosemary

½ teaspoon sea salt

½ teaspoon crushed red pepper (optional)

½ cup extra-virgin olive oil

Shrimp and Chorizo with Latin Flavors

This Spanish-inspired appetizer will be the hit of your party. When you marinate shrimp in lemon juice, the acid from the lemon can actually "cook" the shrimp and change its texture over time. By using only lemon zest here, you can let the shrimp marinate longer, which results in better flavor. These skewers are pretty served warm on a tray with grilled bread, Spanish olives, and Manchego cheese.

SERVES 8 AS AN APPETIZER   HANDS-ON 35 MINUTES
TOTAL 4 HOURS, 35 MINUTES, INCLUDING 4 HOURS CHILLING

2 tablespoons sherry vinegar

3 tablespoons extra-virgin olive oil

½ cup chopped fresh parsley

3 garlic cloves, minced

2 teaspoons lemon zest

¾ teaspoon smoked paprika

½ teaspoon kosher salt

¼ teaspoon black pepper

1 large bay leaf

1 pound large raw shrimp, peeled and deveined

1 (8-ounce) package smoked chorizo (such as Boar's Head)

1. Whisk together the vinegar and next 8 ingredients in a large bowl. Add the shrimp, tossing to coat. Cover and chill 4 hours.

2. Preheat the grill to medium.

3. Drain the shrimp from the marinade, discarding marinade, and season with salt and pepper.

4. Grill the shrimp 3 minutes per side or just until done.

5. Slice the chorizo in half lengthwise, and then slice into ¼-inch-thick slices.

6. To assemble, skewer a chorizo slice followed by a grilled shrimp. Serve immediately.

Negroni

The Negroni originated in Italy and is considered an aperitif, or drink served before a meal to stimulate the appetite. This is one of my favorite drinks, and I prefer it served ice cold, up, but it can be served over ice too. It's got a hint of pleasing bitterness and is so refreshing. One of my favorite memories of this drink is a dinner John and I had with our daughter Emma after she had been in Los Angeles for about a month (our first time seeing her after she moved away from home). We sat outside at this lovely restaurant surrounded by twinkling string lights and the whole thing just felt enchanted. We each had a predinner cocktail—John, a martini, Emma, a glass of Champagne, and a Negroni for me—while we talked and looked over the menu. The conversation and the meal were perfect, and it was just one of those evenings you never forget. I'll always associate this drink with happy memories.

SERVES 1   HANDS-ON 5 MINUTES   TOTAL 5 MINUTES

Stir together the gin, Campari, and sweet vermouth in a rocks or martini glass. Add ice, and garnish with orange peel, if desired, or serve up without ice.

1 ounce gin

1 ounce Campari

1 ounce sweet vermouth

Garnish: orange peel

TIP: You can also mix all ingredients into a cocktail shaker with ice, shake, and strain into a martini glass or Champagne coupe.

Meatballs and Red Sauce

———

One of our favorite restaurants in New York City's Little Italy is called Angelo's of Mulberry Street. They are always happy to see us and treat us like family. The atmosphere is Old World and the food is out of this world! It's a tradition for us on every NYC trip. Their meatballs are so tender and full of flavor. This recipe is the closest I've found. I like to serve these as cicchetti (Italian-style tapas) at a cocktail party. Just arrange the meatballs on top of the sauce in a serving bowl and let guests dig in, breaking off bits of meatball and dipping pieces of sliced ciabatta bread into the sauce. If you want to serve the meatballs American-style with spaghetti for a main course, see the note at the end of the recipe. Enjoy!

**SERVES 8 AS AN APPETIZER   HANDS-ON 1 HOUR, 15 MINUTES
TOTAL 3 HOURS, 15 MINUTES, INCLUDING 2 HOURS CHILLING**

RED SAUCE

¼ cup olive oil

6 garlic cloves, peeled and minced

¼ teaspoon crushed red pepper

2 (28-ounce) cans crushed tomatoes

1 dried bay leaf

1 teaspoon kosher salt

2 teaspoons chopped fresh oregano or
  ¾ teaspoon dried oregano

¼ teaspoon freshly ground black pepper

⅓ cup (packed) fresh basil leaves,
  chopped

MEATBALLS

1 cup roughly torn day-old Italian bread

1 cup whole milk

8 ounces ground beef

8 ounces ground pork

8 ounces ground veal

3 large eggs, beaten

4 garlic cloves, finely chopped

1 cup grated Parmesan cheese

½ cup coarsely chopped fresh parsley

1 teaspoon kosher salt

3 teaspoons chopped fresh oregano or
  1 teaspoon dried oregano

½ teaspoon freshly ground black
  pepper

½ teaspoon fennel seeds

½ teaspoon crushed red pepper

¼ cup olive oil

Grated Parmesan cheese and
  chopped fresh parsley

Thinly sliced ciabatta bread

1. Make the sauce: Heat the oil in a large Dutch oven over medium-low. Add the garlic and crushed red pepper; cook 30 seconds. Add the tomatoes, bay leaf, salt, oregano, and black pepper, and stir. Reduce the heat and gently simmer, stirring occasionally, until the sauce has thickened and the flavors have concentrated, at least 2 and up to 3 hours. Remove and discard the bay leaf, and add the basil.

2. Make the meatballs: While the sauce simmers, combine the bread and milk in a bowl. Let it stand until moistened, about 5 minutes Squeeze the bread with your hands to remove excess milk, and discard the milk. Tear the bread into small, pea-size pieces; return the bread to the bowl.

3. Combine the beef, pork, veal, eggs, garlic, 1 cup Parmesan, ½ cup parsley, 1 teaspoon salt, oregano, black pepper, fennel, and crushed red pepper in a bowl. Using your hands, gently mix in the bread until the ingredients are evenly distributed (do not overmix).

4. Moisten your hands with cool water and roll the meat mixture between your palms into 24 golf-ball-size balls, occasionally moistening hands as needed. Place the meatballs on a rimmed baking sheet, and chill at least 2 hours.

5. Remove the meatballs from fridge. Heat a large skillet over medium-high, and add the oil. Once hot, add the meatballs to the skillet, and cook in batches 3 minutes on each side or until golden brown.

6. Transfer the meatballs to the pot with the tomato sauce. Increase the heat to medium-low, cover, and simmer until the meatballs are cooked through, about 10 to 15 minutes.

7. To serve, spoon the sauce on the bottom of a large rimmed platter. Arrange the meatballs on top. Top with grated cheese and parsley. Serve family-style with a basket of sliced ciabatta bread at the table.

AD LIB

If you want to serve this with spaghetti, just double the sauce and cook spaghetti according to package directions. Drain, reserving 1 cup of the pasta cooking liquid, and return the pasta to the pot over medium-low. Spoon the reserved 1½ cups sauce over the pasta, and toss to coat. Add the pasta cooking liquid, ¼ cup at a time, as needed, to loosen the sauce and coat the pasta. Plate the pasta and top with the meatballs and remaining sauce. Sprinkle with Parmesan and parsley.

Eggplant and Goat Cheese Stacks with Tarragon Tomato Sauce

These are like little eggplant and goat cheese sandwiches (that you eat with a fork). It's a great first course or vegetarian main course that kind of has it all. It's elegant enough for a formal dinner party, but rustic enough for a more low-key occasion. It's a nice combination of crunchy and creamy. The tomato sauce gives it an Italian accent while the tarragon steers it more in the French direction. (Fun fact: Tarragon is one of the four most commonly used herbs in French cooking. The others are parsley, chives, and chervil.)

SERVES 8 AS AN APPETIZER OR 4 AS A MAIN DISH
HANDS-ON 55 MINUTES   TOTAL 1 HOUR, 20 MINUTES

1. Cook the onion in the olive oil in a 3½-quart saucepan over medium 7 to 9 minutes or until softened. Add the tomatoes, tarragon, 1¼ teaspoons salt, sugar, and pepper. Cook over medium, 30 minutes, stirring occasionally.

2. Sprinkle both sides of the eggplant slices with salt; place in a single layer on a layer of paper towels; let stand 30 minutes. Wipe away excess salt; pat dry.

3. Stir together the breadcrumbs and Parmesan. Dip the eggplant slices into the beaten eggs. Coat both sides evenly with the breadcrumb mixture, pressing to adhere.

4. Heat the oil in a large skillet over medium-high. Fry the eggplant 3 minutes per side until golden. Place on a wire rack set over a rimmed baking sheet lined with paper towels.

5. Spread half of the sauce on a serving tray. Arrange a layer of 8 eggplant slices on the tray. Top each eggplant slice with a slice (or crumbles) of goat cheese. Top the goat cheese with another eggplant slice. Drizzle the stacks with the remaining sauce. Garnish with the tarragon, if desired.

TIP: Serve 1 "sandwich" as an appetizer or first course and 2 as a main course.

1 tablespoon olive oil

1 small onion, diced (½ cup)

1 (28-ounce) can crushed tomatoes

1 teaspoon chopped fresh tarragon, plus more for garnish

1¼ teaspoons kosher salt plus more for sprinkling

1 teaspoon sugar

½ teaspoon freshly ground black pepper

1 large eggplant (1¼ pounds), peeled and cut into 16 rounds (about 1 inch thick)

1½ cups panko (Japanese breadcrumbs)

½ cup grated Parmesan cheese

3 large eggs, beaten

1 cup canola oil

8 ounces herbed goat cheese, sliced into 8 rounds, or crumbled

Baked Olive Cheese Dip

This is such a crowd-pleaser! When I make this, it disappears fast. I love that it's easy to make ahead if you're entertaining. Assemble and refrigerate it in advance and then pop it in the oven just before guests arrive. Serve with tortilla chips or your favorite crackers.

SERVES 8   HANDS-ON 25 MINUTES   TOTAL 45 MINUTES

1 (8-ounce) package cream cheese, softened

1 cup grated Parmesan cheese

1 cup shredded pepper Jack cheese

¼ cup mayonnaise

2 garlic cloves, minced

½ cup roughly chopped green olives

½ cup roughly chopped black olives

⅓ cup rinsed, diced pepperoncini peppers

2 green onions, finely chopped (about ¼ cup), plus more for garnish

Crackers, toasted bread slices, or tortilla chips

1. Preheat the oven to 350°F.

2. Beat the cream cheese with a mixer at medium speed 2 minutes. Stir in the Parmesan cheese, pepper Jack, and mayonnaise. Beat at medium speed just until blended. Add the garlic, green olives, black olives, pepperoncini peppers, and green onions, beating just until combined.

3. Transfer to an 8-inch baking dish and bake for 20 to 25 minutes or until golden brown. Serve with crackers, toasted bread slices, or tortilla chips. Garnish with chopped green onions, if desired.

TIP: This can be assembled and refrigerated up to 1 day ahead. Just let it come to room temperature before baking.

AD LIB

This is one recipe that can be made so many ways. Don't like black olives—or any olives for that matter? Leave them out! You're still going to have a delicious spicy cheese dip. I love adding ½ pound of browned hot Italian sausage for a heartier version. This is good warm or cold. I love serving it warm for company, but the next day (if there is any left) I eat it on a cracker right out of the fridge.

For a French Bread Pizza, serve it spread on the cut side of half of a baguette, sliced lengthwise and broiled until melted and bubbly.

Whiskey Smash

To be honest, I had never had a whiskey smash until I was researching cocktails for this chapter. Now it's one of my favorites, and I even made a tray of them for our photography crew to celebrate a great day on the photo shoot for this book. The citrus and mint combo makes this refreshing and easy to drink. Make sure you don't skip the step of muddling the lemons. Really get in there and smash 'em! A lot of the citrus flavor comes from the oils that are released from the lemon peel during muddling.

SERVES 2   HANDS-ON 10 MINUTES   TOTAL 10 MINUTES

1. Muddle the lemon and 8 mint leaves in the bottom of a cocktail shaker. Add the Simple Syrup and bourbon; fill the shaker with ice. Cover with the lid, and shake vigorously until well chilled, about 30 seconds. Strain into 2 rocks glasses filled with crushed ice.

2. Clap or lightly rub 2 mint sprigs between your hands, and place 1 in each glass. Serve with a lemon wedge, if desired.

1 lemon, cut into 8 wedges, plus more for garnish

8 fresh mint leaves plus 2 mint sprigs for garnish

1½ ounces Simple Syrup (page 40)

4 ounces good-quality bourbon

Garnish: lemon wedges

Roasted Maple-Cinnamon Pecans

*I love pecans. I can't stop eating this sweet, salty, cinnamon-spiced version!
The nuts are delicious on their own (um, by the handful), great on salads, and
amazing chopped up finely and sprinkled over ice cream, and they make a sweet
homemade gift for the holidays. BONUS—they take all of 15 minutes to make.*

MAKES 2 CUPS   HANDS-ON 15 MINUTES   TOTAL 15 MINUTES

2 tablespoons coconut sugar

2 tablespoons pure maple
 syrup

½ teaspoon ground cinnamon

¼ teaspoon kosher salt

2 teaspoons coconut oil

2 cups unsalted pecan halves

1. Line a baking sheet with parchment paper or lightly
greased heavy-duty aluminum foil. Set aside.

2. In a small bowl, whisk together the coconut sugar, maple
syrup, cinnamon, and salt.

3. In a large nonstick skillet over medium-low, add the
coconut oil and sugar mixture. Stir until melted and smooth.

4. Add the pecans, and increase the heat to medium, stirring
until the pecans are thoroughly coated.

5. Cook over medium, stirring occasionally, about 3 minutes,
or just until the pecans have absorbed the sugar mixture.

6. Transfer the pecans to the prepared baking sheet, and
spread in a single layer. Let cool completely. Store in an
airtight container up to 2 weeks.

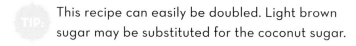

TIP: This recipe can easily be doubled. Light brown
sugar may be substituted for the coconut sugar.

Hot Tea with Lemonade, Bourbon, Cinnamon, and Orange

This started out as an idea for a warm Arnold Palmer. My daughter Delaney was here when I was testing it, and it was her thought to add cinnamon and orange peel. Great idea! This hot toddy hits the spot on a chilly night and is especially warming and therapeutic if you have been nursing a cold.

SERVES 1   HANDS-ON 10 MINUTES   TOTAL 10 MINUTES

Stir together the tea, lemonade, bourbon, and orange peel in a warm heatproof mug. Add the cinnamon stick, stir, and serve immediately.

AD LIB

Try this recipe with different types of tea, such as orange pekoe or lemon-ginger, to create your favorite spin.

1 cup hot brewed Irish breakfast tea (or any black tea)

3 tablespoons prepared refrigerated lemonade, at room temperature

1½ to 2 ounces bourbon

1 (2-inch) strip orange peel

1 (3-inch) cinnamon stick

Irish Coffee

What a delicious way to end a meal or sip by the fire on a cold night! I love Ireland and have been lucky to visit many times. But I don't believe I've ever had an Irish coffee in Ireland, which I think I need to fix by going back as soon as possible. Don't you agree?

SERVES 1   HANDS-ON 10 MINUTES   TOTAL 10 MINUTES

½ cup hot black coffee

2 to 4 teaspoons turbinado
sugar (or sugar in the raw)

2 ounces Irish whiskey
(such as Jameson)

¼ to ⅓ cup heavy cream
(see Tip)

1. Place a stainless-steel spoon in a glass. Pour hot tap water to fill the glass; drain.

2. Pour the hot coffee in the warm glass, filling it about three-fourths full. Stir in the sugar until dissolved. Pour in the whiskey without stirring.

3. Drizzle or "float" the cream slowly over back of the warm spoon, being careful not to break the surface of the coffee, creating a 1½-inch-thick raft. Drink immediately, sipping under the cream for optimum flavor.

TIP: What's the trick to getting the cream to float on top and not sink? I've found that if you whip the cream ever so lightly by hand, not even to soft peaks, just until slightly thickened, it floats more easily.

THE SALADS I REMEMBER HAVING AT DINNER WHEN I WAS A KID were made up of iceberg lettuce with bottled French, Ranch, or blue cheese dressing. Sometimes Mom would add radishes, tomatoes, or green peppers, but that was pretty much the extent of the salad bar in our house! I later found out that iceberg lettuce consists of mostly water (which is good for you, don't get me wrong) but it has a lower nutritional value than darker, leafy greens. Once I was exposed to different kinds of salads (and the versatility of homemade dressings) it was hard to go back to iceberg and a bottle.

These days we have a salad with almost every meal and John, who used to be an iceberg-only guy (smothered in Thousand Island dressing, mind you), loves eating all kinds of salads. Delaney, Emma, and Ava love them too. I really love mixed greens. Plus, eating at least 4 cups of dark leafy greens a day is so good for you! They are loaded with nutrients that help fight cancer, detox your system, and provide you with lots of fiber. Eating that many cups of greens in a day is kind of hard, but I find that when I do, my skin looks great and I just feel better and have more energy overall.

I don't remember when or how salads became so popular, but now they are meals in themselves with seemingly endless variations. In this chapter, I call for an assortment of greens, including kale, romaine, butter lettuce, and spinach. You'll find romaine called for often, as a matter of fact, but you can definitely substitute most any type of lettuce you like. Adding an array of other ingredients to the greens gives a salad flavor, texture, and color. Some of my favorite additions include beets, cheese, watermelon, cucumber, dried cranberries, toasted nuts, Brussels sprouts, broccoli, and cauliflower. And you can always add grilled chicken, salmon, or a few cooked shrimp. I've included some of my favorite salads here for you. Some can be served as sides and some are hearty main courses. I think you'll find there's a little something for everyone here. Who knows? . . . I might just make big-salad lovers out of a few more iceberg diehards yet!

Watermelon, Cucumber, and Tomato Salad with Feta and Fresh Herbs

Growing up we always looked forward to summer because it meant juicy ripe tomatoes, crisp cucumbers, and ice-cold watermelon. The incredible combination of flavors in this refreshing salad—basil, feta, and peppery arugula in a perfectly balanced vinaigrette—wow! It's truly like a flavor explosion bite after bite.

SERVES 6   HANDS-ON 30 MINUTES   TOTAL 30 MINUTES

1 tablespoon white wine vinegar

1 garlic clove, minced

2 tablespoons extra-virgin olive oil

1 tablespoon lemon juice

¼ teaspoon kosher salt

¼ teaspoon freshly ground black pepper

2 tablespoons shredded mint leaves

2 tablespoons shredded basil leaves

3 cups cubed (1-inch chunks) seedless watermelon

1 English cucumber, peeled and cut into 1-inch chunks (about 2 cups)

1 cup halved cherry tomatoes

1 (5-ounce) package baby arugula (about 5½ cups) (optional)

½ cup crumbled feta

Whisk together the vinegar, garlic, olive oil, lemon juice, salt, and pepper in a large bowl. Stir in the mint and basil. Add the watermelon, cucumber, and tomatoes, tossing to coat. Add the arugula, if desired, and feta, tossing gently to combine.

NOTE: Two Kumatoes (brown heirloom tomatoes) may be substituted for the cherry tomatoes. Cut them lengthwise into sixths and then in half again.

AD LIB

This is great as a side salad with grilled meats or just enjoyed all on its own. You could make it more of a main dish by adding grilled shrimp.

Romaine Salad with Buttermilk Parmesan Dressing

I don't know about you but when I use buttermilk in a recipe I always end up with tons left over. (Can we discuss why they won't sell it in smaller containers?) Well, this dressing is a great way to use what's left of it. This is a tasty dressing that brings crisp lettuce like romaine to life. I love this salad with grilled meat.

SERVES 6 TO 8   **HANDS-ON 20 MINUTES**   **TOTAL 20 MINUTES**

1. Whisk together the buttermilk, Parmesan, mayonnaise, vinegar, parsley, chives, Dijon, Worcestershire, and hot sauce in a medium bowl. Season to taste with salt and freshly ground black pepper.

2. Toss the dressing with the lettuce just before serving. Garnish with a bit of cracked black pepper, if desired.

TIP: If you want a thicker dressing with more body, increase the mayonnaise to about ¼ cup.

½ cup buttermilk

3 tablespoons grated Parmesan or Romano cheese

2 tablespoons mayonnaise

2 tablespoons white wine vinegar

2 tablespoons minced fresh parsley

1 tablespoon minced chives

½ teaspoon Dijon mustard

⅛ teaspoon Worcestershire sauce

⅛ teaspoon hot sauce

Kosher salt and freshly ground black pepper

1 large head romaine lettuce (8 cups chopped or torn)

Garnish: cracked black pepper

Broccoli and Cauliflower Salad

I love this salad! It's full of flavor and crunchy texture. It does make a large salad, which is great for a potluck. If you want a smaller version, just halve the recipe, even though you can munch on it for a few days straight out of the refrigerator. And trust me, you'll want to.

SERVES 12 TO 16   HANDS-ON 40 MINUTES
TOTAL 1 HOUR, 40 MINUTES, INCLUDING CHILLING TIME

¾ cup plain Greek yogurt

½ cup mayonnaise

¼ cup honey

2 tablespoons red wine vinegar

1 tablespoon sugar

¼ teaspoon kosher salt, or more to taste

4 cups small diced broccoli florets (about 1½ pounds)

4 cups small diced cauliflower florets (about 2 pounds)

8 slices bacon, diced and cooked

2 shallots, diced (½ cup)

½ cup sweetened dried cranberries

½ cup chopped toasted pecans (see page 106)

Whisk together the yogurt, mayonnaise, honey, vinegar, sugar, and salt in a large bowl. Stir in the broccoli, cauliflower, bacon, shallots, cranberries, and pecans, tossing to coat. Cover and chill 1 hour.

TIP: The dressing and salad can be made and stored separately 1 day ahead. Add the dressing 1 hour before serving to allow the flavors to really come together.

Romaine Salad with Pear, Smoked Blue Cheese, and Candied Pecans

As you may have noticed by now, I'm a fan of smoked cheeses. Smoked Gouda, smoked mozzarella, smoked Cheddar, and I really love smoked blue cheese. I first had it just last year at a restaurant in Nashville and was blown away. (I actually tracked down the chef and asked what kind it was.) The smoking seems to me to tame that strong bite, which makes it milder and easier to eat. I've been known to eat it by the chunk . . . yep, just pop it right in my mouth!

This salad combines many of my favorite flavors: pears, romaine lettuce, candied pecans, and blue cheese. These flavors work well in the fall, but it's really delicious any time of year.

SERVES 6   HANDS-ON 20 MINUTES   TOTAL 35 MINUTES

1. Cook the sugar and pecans in a small skillet over medium, 5 to 7 minutes or until the sugar has caramelized. Spread the pecans in a single layer on lightly greased wax paper on a large baking sheet. Let them cool completely and then chop into ½-inch pieces.

2. Whisk together the olive oil, vinegar, Dijon, garlic, salt, sugar, and pepper in a small bowl.

3. Layer the lettuce, pears, cheese, avocado, and green onions on a large serving platter.

4. Drizzle with the desired amount of dressing, and top with the pecans.

¼ cup sugar

½ cup pecan halves

⅓ cup extra-virgin olive oil

3 tablespoons red wine vinegar

1½ teaspoons Dijon mustard

1 garlic clove, minced

½ teaspoon kosher salt

½ teaspoon sugar

¼ teaspoon black pepper

2 romaine hearts, torn (about 6 cups)

2 ripe pears, thinly sliced or chopped (about ¾ cup)

5 ounces smoked blue cheese, crumbled

1 avocado, diced

4 thinly sliced green onions (about ½ cup)

AD LIB

This salad is so versatile that you can really make it your own. If you can't find smoked blue cheese, regular works just as well. Or, if you don't like blue cheese, substitute feta or goat cheese, or go cheeseless! If you're watching sugar, skip it, and just toast the pecans in the oven for a few minutes until they are lightly crunchy and fragrant. Chopped cooked bacon or pancetta is also a nice addition. Use the Roasted Maple-Cinnamon Pecans (page 82) for a change of pace.

Boston Lettuce Simple Salad

A simple vinaigrette recipe is always good to have on hand. My father-in-law made the best vinaigrette. I asked him how to do it and he showed me once, but I didn't write it down and so . . . it's gone. But I think this comes pretty close. Boston lettuce is so fluffy and fresh. It's a favorite of mine.

SERVES 4   HANDS-ON 10 MINUTES   TOTAL 10 MINUTES

2 tablespoons white wine
   vinegar
1 small shallot, diced (about
   3 tablespoons)
½ teaspoon Dijon mustard
¼ teaspoon kosher salt
Freshly ground black pepper
3 tablespoons extra-virgin
   olive oil
1 head Boston lettuce, torn

1. Whisk together the vinegar, shallots, Dijon, salt, and pepper in a medium bowl. Add the oil in a slow, steady stream, whisking until smooth.

2. Drizzle desired amount of the dressing over the lettuce on serving plates.

AD LIB

You could add chopped cooked bacon and fresh tomatoes to this if you want something a little heartier.

Thai Slaw with Peanut Dressing

———

This is all about the crunch and the dressing. I've always loved this kind of salad, and writing this book gave me the motivation I needed to figure out my ideal recipe. Yes, there is a bit of sugar in the dressing but overall this salad is full of good-for-you ingredients. Trust me, the dressing is key to this slaw's yummy goodness. I can't think of any other way to put it!

SERVES 6 TO 8   HANDS-ON 35 MINUTES   TOTAL 35 MINUTES

1. Whisk together the peanut butter, brown sugar, lime juice, honey, soy sauce, sesame oil, Sriracha, ginger, and garlic in a medium bowl. Set aside.

2. Cook the edamame according to the package directions. Let cool slightly.

3. Stir together the edamame, cabbage, carrots, bell pepper, green onions, and cilantro in a large bowl. Stir in the peanut dressing, tossing to coat. Top with the peanuts and sesame seeds just before serving.

AD LIB

This dressing would make a delicious sauce for chilled grilled chicken or kabobs. Or as a dipping sauce for the little one's (and let's face it, sometimes the big one's) chicken fingers. Speaking of chicken, grill up a boneless, skinless breast and toss it in this salad for added protein.

⅓ cup creamy peanut butter

1½ tablespoons brown sugar

2 tablespoons lime juice

2 tablespoons honey

1½ tablespoons soy sauce

1½ teaspoons sesame oil

1 teaspoon Sriracha

1-inch piece ginger, peeled and grated

1 large garlic clove, finely chopped

1 cup frozen shelled edamame

6 cups shredded cabbage (half of a 2-pound, 5-ounce head of cabbage)

2 carrots, shredded (1 cup)

1 red bell pepper, cut into thin strips (1½ cups)

2 green onions, thinly sliced (½ cup)

⅓ cup chopped fresh cilantro

¼ cup salted peanuts, chopped or whole

Sesame seeds

DON'T KNOCK IT 'TIL YOU TRY IT

We had this "salad" at every family gathering and holiday when I was growing up, and I still make it for Thanksgiving and Christmas. I'm fully aware of how strange this recipe sounds, but it's just part of my heritage, so I wanted to share it with you. It's sweet and fluffy and, admittedly, a lot more like a dessert than a salad.

Fluff Salad

SERVES 10   HANDS-ON 10 MINUTES   TOTAL 10 MINUTES

1 (5-ounce) jar pimiento cheese spread (Kraft)

1 (8-ounce) can pineapple tidbits, drained

½ (10.5-ounce) bag miniature marshmallows (about 3 ⅓ cups)

1 (8-ounce) container frozen whipped topping, thawed

Stir together the cheese spread and pineapple in a large bowl. Add the marshmallows, stirring well to combine. Fold in the whipped topping, and mix well. Serve immediately, or cover and refrigerate overnight.

TIP: The key to this is mixing, mixing, mixing. Mix until you think it's mixed, and then mix it some more! You will see it getting fluffier and more cohesive. I find it's best if made the night before and refrigerated.

Cranberry, Avocado, and Spinach Salad with Orange-Poppy Seed Dressing

I call this a "bang-for-your-buck" kind of recipe. You get lots of variations, all covered with this delicious dressing. This salad and dressing are fresh and light and packed with healthy, flavorful ingredients. Serves eight as a side salad or four as a main course topped with chicken, salmon, or shrimp. I'm really happy that Delaney, my oldest, has developed a love of cooking. She started cooking professionally this year, cooking for a personal chef company here in Nashville. It's great for us to be able to have a shared interest in something we both love. When I was testing recipes for this book I would sometimes give her recipes to make to help me out. She made this salad for one of our family dinners and it was amazing. (I also enjoyed being cooked for for a change!) You will have extra dressing left over, which may be stored in the refrigerator for several days.

SERVES 4   HANDS-ON 25 MINUTES   TOTAL 25 MINUTES

2 teaspoons orange zest

¼ cup freshly squeezed orange juice

2 tablespoons fresh lemon juice

2 tablespoons honey

2 teaspoons Dijon mustard

¼ teaspoon kosher salt

1 tablespoon poppy seeds

½ cup extra-virgin olive oil

1 (6-ounce) package fresh baby spinach (about 4 cups)

½ cup crumbled feta cheese

⅓ cup sliced toasted almonds

¼ cup sweetened dried cranberries

1 medium-size ripe avocado, sliced

1. Whisk together the zest, juices, honey, Dijon, salt, and poppy seeds in a small bowl. Slowly drizzle the oil into the citrus mixture, whisking constantly until well blended.

2. Place the spinach in a large bowl. Sprinkle with the cheese, almonds, cranberries, and avocado. Drizzle with the desired amount of vinaigrette, and toss gently to coat. Serve immediately.

Toasting Nuts: Preheat the oven to 350°F. Bake the nuts in a single layer in a shallow pan 5 to 7 minutes or until lightly toasted and fragrant, stirring halfway through.

variations

Grilled Chicken: 2 skinless, boneless chicken breasts • ½ teaspoon kosher salt ¼ teaspoon black pepper • 1 tablespoon olive oil. Preheat a charcoal grill to medium-high (about 450°F), or use a grill pan. Season the chicken with the salt and pepper. Rub the oil evenly over the chicken. Grill the chicken 6 minutes on each side or until done. Slice and serve over the Cranberry, Avocado, and Spinach Salad. Serves 4

Blackened Salmon: 4 (4-ounce) salmon fillets • 1½ teaspoons Old Bay with Blackened Seasoning • 2 teaspoons canola oil. Sprinkle the seasoning over the fish. Heat oil in a 10-inch cast-iron skillet over high just until the skillet begins to smoke. Remove the pan from the heat; add the salmon, flesh side down. Return to the heat, and reduce the heat to medium-high. Cook 4 minutes. Turn the fish and cook until the skin is crispy, about 4 minutes more. Remove the skin. Serve over the Cranberry, Avocado, and Spinach Salad. Serves 4

Blackened Shrimp: ¾ pound large shrimp • 1 teaspoon Old Bay with Blackened Seasoning • 1 teaspoon canola oil. Sprinkle the seasoning over the shrimp. Heat oil in a 10-inch cast-iron skillet over high just until the skillet begins to smoke. Remove the pan from the heat; add the shrimp. Return to the heat, and reduce the heat to medium-high. Cook 1 minute. Turn the shrimp, and cook until they turn pink, 1 to 2 minutes more. Serve over the Cranberry, Avocado, and Spinach Salad. Serves 4

Shredded Brussels Sprouts Salad with Maple-Balsamic Vinaigrette

If you want to get your kids to eat Brussels sprouts, this may be the way to do it. Ava hated them, but didn't recognize them in this salad. With its sweet-and-tangy dressing and crunchy pecans, she cleaned her plate. Frankly, I like to eat this by the bowlful, but it also makes a great side salad or starter. Feel free to add two to three slices of chopped, cooked smoked bacon.

SERVES 6 TO 8 • HANDS-ON 30 MINUTES • TOTAL 30 MINUTES

1. Whisk together the olive oil, vinegar, maple syrup, and Dijon in a medium bowl. Season to taste with salt and freshly ground black pepper.

2. Thinly slice the Brussels sprouts, discarding core. Stir together the Brussels sprouts, sliced shallot, dried cranberries, pecans, Gorgonzola cheese, and chopped pear.

3. Pour the dressing over the salad, and gently toss to combine. Serve immediately.

2 tablespoons extra-virgin olive oil

2 tablespoons balsamic vinegar

1 tablespoon pure maple syrup

1 teaspoon Dijon mustard

Kosher salt and freshly ground black pepper

12 ounces Brussels sprouts, tough outer leaves pulled away (about 3 cups)

1 medium shallot, thinly sliced (about $\frac{1}{4}$ cup)

$\frac{1}{4}$ cup sweetened dried cranberries

$\frac{1}{4}$ cup coarsely chopped pecans

$\frac{1}{4}$ cup crumbled Gorgonzola cheese

1 ripe pear, chopped (about $\frac{3}{4}$ cup)

Kale Caesar Salad with Quinoa and Chicken

There is a restaurant in Nashville called Tavern that has a kale Caesar salad that I love. This is my rendition, only with the addition of healthy fiber and protein in the form of quinoa. Lemon, freshly grated Parmesan, and toasted walnuts take this salad over the top. For a variation, you can try this topped with the Blackened Salmon on page 107 or keep this meatless if you prefer.

SERVES 4   HANDS-ON 25 MINUTES   TOTAL 25 MINUTES

¼ cup uncooked quinoa

2 tablespoons hot water

2 tablespoons mayonnaise

1½ tablespoons extra-virgin olive oil

1 tablespoon freshly squeezed lemon juice

¼ teaspoon freshly ground black pepper

1 garlic clove, minced

6 tablespoons grated Parmesan cheese

5 cups finely chopped, stemmed, Lacinato kale (from a 7¼-ounce bunch)

1½ cups chopped skinless rotisserie chicken

2 tablespoons chopped toasted walnuts (see page 106)

1. Cook the quinoa according to the package directions. Let cool slightly.

2. Whisk together the water, mayonnaise, olive oil, lemon juice, pepper, and garlic in a large bowl. Stir in 3 tablespoons of the Parmesan cheese. Add the kale, quinoa, and chicken, tossing to coat.

3. Transfer to a serving platter, and top with the remaining 3 tablespoons Parmesan cheese and walnuts.

Salmon Salad with Parmesan Croutons

Growing up in landlocked Kansas, we didn't have a lot of access to fresh seafood, and we rarely ate anything other than bass or trout that we caught from our pond, so I just started eating salmon a few years ago. Now I'm kind of obsessed. I love it, plus it's so good for you since it's rich in omega-3, which is important for heart health. I especially love it on salads, like this flavorful one. I'm not usually a crouton girl, but the Parmesan makes these irresistible.

SERVES 4   HANDS-ON 40 MINUTES   TOTAL 1 HOUR

1. Preheat the oven to 450°F.

2. Slice the baguette into ½-inch cubes, and toss with 1½ tablespoons of the olive oil, a pinch of salt and pepper, and 1 tablespoon of the Parmesan cheese. Transfer to a large lightly greased rimmed baking sheet. Bake 7 to 9 minutes or until browned and crispy, stirring halfway through. Let cool.

3. Place the cabbage in a medium bowl. Stir in 2 tablespoons of the lemon juice and 1 tablespoon of the olive oil. Season with salt and black pepper. Let stand, stirring occasionally, for at least 10 minutes.

4. Pat the salmon fillets dry with paper towels. Season with a bit of salt and black pepper. Heat 2 tablespoons of the olive oil in a large skillet. Add the fish, skin side down. Cook 4 to 6 minutes or until the flesh is opaque and the skin is crispy. Turn and cook 1 to 2 minutes or to the desired degree of doneness. Transfer to a cutting board. When cool enough to handle, remove and discard the skin. Flake the fish into chunks and set aside to cool, 5 minutes.

5. Whisk together the mayonnaise, remaining 1 tablespoon cheese and 2 tablespoons lemon juice, and the garlic. Slowly whisk in the remaining 2 tablespoons olive oil until combined. Season with salt and black pepper to taste.

6. Drain the cabbage. In a large bowl, combine the lettuce, flaked salmon, marinated cabbage, and Parmesan croutons. Add enough dressing to coat, and gently toss thoroughly to combine. Garnish with the basil, if desired.

1 (8-ounce) baguette

6½ tablespoons extra-virgin olive oil

Kosher salt and freshly ground black pepper

2 tablespoons grated Parmesan cheese

½ small head red cabbage, cored and thinly sliced

4 tablespoons fresh lemon juice

4 skin-on salmon fillets (about 1 pound)

¼ cup mayonnaise

2 garlic cloves, minced

1 head baby romaine lettuce or romaine lettuce hearts, torn (about 6 cups)

Garnish: 6 to 8 torn fresh basil leaves

Roasted Beet, Goat Cheese, and Walnut Salad

I love beets! I know they aren't for everyone, but if you even just barely like beets I encourage you to try this salad. With the thyme, goat cheese, and walnuts, this is the kind of salad you find on a high-end restaurant menu. It's that good and so pretty any season of the year. While beets are a cool-season crop, they are available all year at the supermarket. Make this in the spring or summer to serve alongside grilled pork chops or simple fish, or make it a side salad for a winter dinner party or holiday meal. Your friends and family will be impressed.

SERVES 4 TO 6   HANDS-ON 35 MINUTES   TOTAL 1 HOUR, 10 MINUTES

6 medium beets (2 bunches, about 2 pounds)

2 garlic cloves, pressed

½ teaspoon chopped fresh thyme

2 teaspoons plus 1 tablespoon red wine vinegar

½ cup plus 1 tablespoon extra-virgin olive oil

3 tablespoons walnut oil

Kosher salt and freshly ground black pepper

1 cup baby arugula

½ cup crumbled goat cheese

⅓ cup chopped toasted walnuts (see page 106)

Garnish: cracked black pepper

1. Preheat the oven to 350°F.

2. Trim the beet stems to 1 inch; gently wash, and place in a lightly greased 13- x 9-inch baking dish with the garlic and thyme. Drizzle with 2 teaspoons of the red wine vinegar and 1 tablespoon of the olive oil. Pour ¼ cup water in the bottom of the dish.

3. Bake the beets, covered with heavy-duty aluminum foil, for 40 to 45 minutes or until tender. Let cool slightly. Peel the beets, and cut into 1-inch cubes.

4. Whisk together the remaining 1 tablespoon red wine vinegar, remaining ½ cup olive oil, and the walnut oil in a small bowl, whisking well. Season to taste with salt and black pepper. Stir in the warm beets, tossing to coat.

5. Place the arugula on a large serving platter. Arrange the beets over the center, and sprinkle with the cheese, walnuts, and a bit of cracked black pepper, if desired. Serve immediately.

 TIP: Don't let the beets cool too long or they will be hard to peel.

Chipotle Chicken Taco Salad

If you want this main course salad to have a little more kick, just up the minced chipotle chiles to taste. Use a cooked rotisserie chicken or grill the chicken breasts on a grill pan on the stove if you don't have, or want to fire up, an outdoor grill. Layering this salad is pretty, but feel free to just toss it together in a big bowl.

SERVES 4 TO 6   HANDS-ON 40 MINUTES   TOTAL 40 MINUTES, INCLUDING DRESSING

1. Preheat a grill to medium-high (about 450°F). Coat a cold cooking grate with cooking spray, and place on the grill. Place the corn on the cooking grate, and grill, covered, 12 minutes, turning every 2 to 3 minutes or until done. Let stand 5 minutes (see Tip).

2. Season the chicken with the salt and pepper. Grill the chicken, covered, 5 minutes on each side or until done.

3. Cut the kernels from the cobs. Discard the cobs. Chop the chicken into 1-inch cubes.

4. Combine the lettuce, tomatoes, avocado, red onion, and black beans on a large serving platter. Top with the grilled corn and chicken. Drizzle with the desired amount of Chipotle Dressing.

TIP: In lieu of grilling the corn, you can remove the kernels from the cob and cook them over medium in a grill pan or skillet until charred and tender.

2 ears fresh corn, husks removed

2 boneless, skinless chicken breasts (1 pound)

½ teaspoon kosher salt

¼ teaspoon black pepper

8 cups chopped romaine lettuce (about 16 ounces)

1 cup halved cherry tomatoes

1 avocado, chopped (about ½ cup)

½ medium-size red onion, thinly sliced (about ⅓ cup)

1 (15-ounce) can black beans, drained and rinsed

Chipotle Dressing (recipe follows)

Chipotle Dressing

⅔ cup light sour cream (plain yogurt may be substituted)

1 tablespoon minced canned chipotle pepper in adobo sauce

4 teaspoons lime juice

1 teaspoon chili powder

1 teaspoon ground cumin

⅓ cup chopped fresh cilantro

¼ teaspoon kosher salt

Mix together the sour cream, chipotle peppers, lime juice, chili powder, cumin, cilantro, and salt in a jar with a tight-fitting lid; shake vigorously to blend. Makes about ¾ cup

MARTINA'S KITCHEN MIX

SOUPS & SANDWICHES

SOUP IS ONE OF MY FAVORITE THINGS TO MAKE, and to eat. It's just about as close as you can get to the perfect food. It's nourishing, warming, hearty, and full of savory ingredients that make you feel like you are taking care of both body and soul. Putting together ingredients that you know are going to give comfort and then letting them simmer on the stove until all the flavors meld and become one flavor seems a little like magic! I always feel like I'm really doing my job as a caretaker for my friends and family when I make soup. I've made it for my kids (and taken it to friends) when they are sick. I've cooked it up for a crowd and let them help themselves from the stove or the slow cooker. Soup is easy to put in a thermos and take on a picnic or to the office, making it the perfect portable lunch. And it's easy to make ahead and often gets better the next day.

Pair it with its partner-in-crime—the sandwich—and you've got everything you need to feel satisfied. I still remember eating fried bologna sandwiches as a kid. It was just white bread, mayo, and fried bologna. Or, if you weren't in the mood to fry it, you put Lay's classic potato chips on top of the bologna on a slice of white bread slathered with mayo, smushed them down with the top piece of bread, and you end up with one of my dad's favorites.

Everyone is so health conscious now . . . and, don't get me wrong, I'm totally behind that. I don't eat sandwiches every day but sometimes a good ol' bologna or PB&J sandwich just does the trick. Sandwiches have gotten a bad rap because of the carbs in the bread. But, as I've said, I believe in balance and sometimes I wonder if the pendulum has swung a bit too far in one direction to the point where we are all afraid of a couple of slices of bread! Give in and try the Blackberry-Bacon Grilled Cheese (page 138) in this chapter. It is a delicious sweet-and-smoky take on a classic grilled cheese. My Chicken Panini with Southwestern Pesto (page 142) is a meal in itself, but is a perfect partner for pretty much any of the soups you will find here.

If any chapter in this book could be classified as a comfort food chapter, this one is it. So go on, get out your big soup pot and cook up a batch of soup and make some sandwiches. You'll be happy you did.

Cream of Tomato Soup

My youngest, Ava, loves this soup! I found it in a kids' cookbook and altered it a little. I've tried a lot of tomato soup recipes and this is one of the best I've tasted. I like the kick the crushed red pepper adds to it, but you can leave it out or use less or more, depending on your taste. I make up a big batch of this and freeze it in small single-serving containers so Ava easily can just warm one up as an after-school snack or weekend lunch. Serve this with a classic grilled cheese or Blackberry-Bacon Grilled Cheese (page 138) and you have a comforting meal.

MAKES 6 ½ CUPS   HANDS-ON 15 MINUTES   TOTAL 55 MINUTES

2 tablespoons olive oil

1 medium yellow onion, diced (about ¾ cup)

2 to 3 cloves garlic, minced (about 1 tablespoon)

¼ to ½ teaspoon crushed red pepper (optional)

4 cups chicken broth

1 (14.5-ounce) can diced tomatoes

1 teaspoon kosher salt

½ teaspoon black pepper

¾ cup heavy whipping cream

1 tablespoon sugar

2 tablespoons butter

Garnish: sliced fresh basil

1. Heat the olive oil in a large saucepan over medium. Cook the onion, stirring often, until soft, 5 to 7 minutes. Add the garlic, and cook 30 seconds to 1 minute longer, stirring occasionally. Stir in the crushed red pepper, if desired, and cook for 1 minute. Add the chicken broth, tomatoes, salt, and pepper. Cook over medium for 35 minutes, stirring occasionally.

2. Remove from the heat, and process the mixture in a blender or with a handheld blender (immersion blender) until smooth.

3. Stir in the cream, sugar, and butter. (The soup may be made to this point, cooled, covered, and refrigerated for a couple days or frozen up to 1 month.) Cook over low until heated through, about 5 minutes. Garnish, if desired.

TIP: If you don't have an immersion blender, a regular blender will work. Just don't fill it more than halfway and be sure to cover the lid with a towel and hold it down tightly. Hot liquids expand, so if you don't do these things, you might end up, at worst, burned, and at best . . . well, no, there really isn't a best-case scenario here, just a big mess and a tomato soup-covered kitchen!

Very Green Broccoli Soup

———

I'm lucky that my kids love vegetables. Broccoli, in particular, is Ava's favorite. This is one of the healthiest and most delicious soups I make. Eating it makes you feel like you are doing something really good for your body and soul. The lemon zest added at the end of cooking really brightens up the flavor. Serve topped with my Gremolata on page 252 for even more of a flavorful burst.

SERVES 4 TO 6   HANDS-ON 25 MINUTES   TOTAL 45 MINUTES

1. Cut the broccoli florets from the stems.

2. Heat the olive oil and butter in a large Dutch oven over medium-high. Add the onion and celery; lower the heat to medium, and season with salt. Cook the vegetables until tender, about 10 minutes. (Adjust the heat so that the vegetables cook without taking on color.) Stir in the minced garlic and thyme. Add the broccoli florets, broth, and salt and pepper to taste. Bring to a boil. Reduce the heat, and simmer until the broccoli is tender, about 7 minutes. Stir in the spinach and lemon zest. Cook just until the spinach wilts. Let cool slightly.

3. Process the mixture in a blender until smooth. (The soup may be made to this point, cooled, covered, and refrigerated for a couple days or frozen up to 1 month.)

4. Cook over low 2 minutes or just until warmed. Stir in the cream. Season to taste with the salt and pepper. Add additional lemon zest to taste if needed. Ladle into serving bowls and sprinkle each serving with a bit of Martina's Gremolata. Serve immediately.

TIP: Fill a blender just half way with hot liquids and cover with a towel. Hot liquids expand and can scald if they escape.

1½ pounds broccoli (about 3½ cups)

2 tablespoons olive oil

1 tablespoon butter

1½ medium onions, diced (about 1 cup)

2 celery stalks, diced (½ cup)

Kosher salt

3 garlic cloves (1 tablespoon), minced

2 teaspoons finely chopped fresh thyme

5 cups chicken broth

Freshly ground black pepper

2 cups packed spinach

2 teaspoons lemon zest plus more to taste

1 cup heavy cream or buttermilk (if using buttermilk, cut the lemon zest in half)

¼ cup Martina's Gremolata (page 252)

Quick-and-Easy White Bean and Baby Greens Stew

This is super quick and easy (hence the title). I've made this more than once after coming home late from the studio and needing to get a comforting, nourishing meal on the table fast. It's hearty and healthy, and I always feel like a good mom when I serve it!

SERVES 6   HANDS-ON 25 MINUTES   TOTAL 30 MINUTES

2 large garlic cloves, chopped

2 tablespoons olive oil

1 (14.5-ounce) can petite-diced or crushed tomatoes, undrained

3½ cups chicken broth

2 (19-ounce) cans cannellini beans, drained and rinsed

1½-pound piece baked ham (½ to ¾ inch thick), cut into ½-inch cubes

¼ teaspoon black pepper

1 (5-ounce) bag baby greens of your choice (baby spinach, baby arugula, baby kale), chopped

12 (¾-inch-thick) slices baguette, toasted

Cook the garlic in the olive oil in a heavy soup pot over medium-high, stirring, about 1 minute. Add the tomatoes (with juice). Stir in the broth, beans, ham, and pepper; bring to a boil. Reduce the heat to low, and simmer, uncovered, 5 minutes. Stir in the greens and cook just until wilted. Top each serving with 2 toasted baguette slices.

TIP: For a zestier flavor, rub the toasted baguette slices with the cut side of a halved garlic clove, or brush with olive oil and sprinkle with Martina's Gremolata on page 252.

AD LIB

If you're a vegetarian, just omit the ham and substitute vegetable broth for the chicken broth.

Creamy Chicken Tortilla Soup

Flavorful and delicious, this is a creamy, comforting version of the classic. Make it spicier by adding more jalapeño or smokier with chipotle chili powder in place of the regular chili powder. I prefer fresh corn here, but frozen will do in a pinch.

SERVES 8   HANDS-ON 45 MINUTES   TOTAL 1 HOUR, 40 MINUTES

1¼ pounds boneless, skinless chicken breasts
1 teaspoon kosher salt
½ teaspoon black pepper
4 cups (32 ounces) chicken broth
1 tablespoon canola oil
1 medium yellow onion, chopped
1 jalapeño, seeded and chopped
3 garlic cloves, chopped
1 teaspoon chili powder
1 teaspoon ground cumin
1 teaspoon paprika
1 (14.5-ounce) can tomatoes with diced green chiles, undrained

⅓ cup masa harina
1⅓ cups milk
1 (15-ounce) can black beans, drained and rinsed
1 (16-ounce) can pinto beans, drained and rinsed
1 cup fresh or frozen corn
⅔ cup heavy cream
⅓ cup sour cream
Garnishes: shredded cheese, sour cream, diced avocado, cilantro, lime wedges, corn tortilla chips, hot sauce

1. Preheat the oven to 350°F. Season the chicken with salt and pepper. Place in a greased 11- x 7-inch baking dish. Pour 1 cup of the broth over the top and cover. Bake 45 minutes or until done. Remove the chicken, reserving the cooking liquid. Shred the meat with 2 forks.

2. Heat the oil in a large Dutch oven over medium-high. Add the onion and jalapeño; cook 3 minutes. Add the garlic; cook 30 seconds, stirring constantly. Add the remaining 3 cups broth, reserved cooking liquid, chili powder, cumin, paprika, and tomatoes.

3. Whisk together the masa and milk until blended. Stir into the soup. Cook over medium-high, stirring frequently, 10 minutes or until the mixture boils and thickens slightly. Stir in the chicken, black beans, pinto beans, and corn. Reduce the heat to low. Stir in the cream and sour cream. Serve with the desired garnishes.

TIP: This is a great recipe for entertaining a group. Set up a toppings bar so guests can help themselves and add their own toppings. Look for masa harina in the ethnic aisle of most supermarkets. It's made from cornmeal treated with slaked lime. Finely ground dry corn tortillas may be substituted in a pinch.

Lasagna Soup

If you're expecting a crowd, this is a fun, filling alternative to chili. It's a yummy new addition to any Super Bowl party repertoire too. As a matter of fact, I made it for our annual Super Bowl party this year, and not only did it quickly disappear, but I had several requests for the recipe. I promise, you will too.

SERVES 10 TO 12   HANDS-ON 45 MINUTES   TOTAL 1 HOUR, 15 MINUTES

2 teaspoons olive oil

1½ pounds ground spicy Italian sausage

3 medium onions, chopped (about 2 cups)

4 garlic cloves, minced

2 teaspoons dried oregano (or 2 tablespoons chopped fresh oregano)

½ teaspoon crushed red pepper

2 tablespoons tomato paste

1 (28-ounce) can fire-roasted diced tomatoes, undrained

2 bay leaves

6 cups chicken broth

½ pound (8 ounces) small orecchiette pasta or elbow macaroni

½ cup finely chopped fresh basil leaves

2 cups shredded mozzarella cheese

½ cup grated Parmesan cheese

Kosher salt and freshly ground black pepper (optional)

1. Heat the olive oil in a large Dutch oven over medium. Add the sausage, breaking up into bite-size pieces; brown for about 5 minutes. Add the onions, and cook until softened, about 6 minutes. Add the garlic, oregano, and crushed red pepper, and cook 1 minute. Add the tomato paste, and stir well. Cook for 3 to 4 minutes or until the tomato paste turns a rusty brown.

2. Stir in the diced tomatoes, bay leaves, and chicken broth. Bring to a boil; reduce the heat, and simmer for 30 minutes. Cook the pasta according to the package directions. Stir into the soup. Stir in the basil.

3. Stir together the mozzarella and Parmesan. Taste the soup and season with salt and pepper, if desired. Discard the bay leaves.

4. To serve, ladle the soup into individual bowls, and top with the cheese mixture.

TIP: Don't cook the soup too long or let it boil after adding the pasta or it will get mushy as it absorbs the broth. You may want to consider cooking the pasta separately, and then adding some to individual bowls before ladling the soup over it. This is especially helpful if you anticipate any leftovers. Buy ground Italian sausage instead of links for this recipe, so you're not stuck removing the meat from the casings.

Cream of Chicken and Wild Rice Soup

Two soups in one! That's what you get with this recipe. If you stop after Step 5, before adding the flour and cream, you will have a delicious, brothy chicken and wild rice soup—the kind you crave on a cold day or when you're down with a cold. The creamy version is thick, velvety, and rich—three words I like in a soup description!

SERVES 8   HANDS-ON 30 MINUTES   TOTAL 1 HOUR

1. Preheat the oven to 350°F.

2. Season the chicken breast with the salt and pepper. Transfer to an 11- x 7-inch baking dish; pour 1 cup of the chicken broth over the chicken, and cover tightly with aluminum foil. Bake for 35 to 40 minutes or until done; reserve the chicken broth for the soup.

3. Prepare the rice according to package directions.

4. Melt 1 tablespoon of the butter over medium in a large Dutch oven. Add the onion, carrots, and celery, and sauté until slightly tender, about 4 minutes, adding the garlic during the last 30 seconds. Add the reserved chicken broth and remaining 3½ cups chicken broth, thyme, marjoram, sage, and rosemary. Season with salt and black pepper. Shred or chop the cooked chicken, and add to the soup. Simmer 15 minutes.

5. Add the cooked rice. (At this point you could stop and have a delicious, healthy, low-fat version of chicken and wild rice soup.)

6. Melt the remaining 6 tablespoons butter in a small saucepan over medium. Add the flour, and cook 1½ minutes, whisking constantly. Gradually whisk in the milk. Cook, stirring constantly, until thickened, about 5 minutes. Add to the soup mixture in the pot, and cook about 5 more minutes or until the soup is thickened. Stir in the heavy cream and lemon zest. Garnish with torn fresh parsley leaves and a bit more lemon zest, if desired. Serve warm.

1 pound boneless, skinless cooked chicken breast halves (the white meat of a rotisserie chicken may be substituted)

Kosher salt and freshly ground black pepper

4½ cups chicken broth

1 cup long-grain and wild rice blend

7 tablespoons butter, diced

2 medium yellow onions, chopped (about 1 cup)

2 large carrots, diced (about 1 cup)

3 medium celery stalks, diced (about 1 cup)

1 garlic clove, minced

¼ teaspoon each dried thyme, marjoram, sage, and rosemary

½ cup all-purpose flour

1½ cups milk

½ cup heavy cream

1 teaspoon lemon zest

Garnishes: fresh parsley leaves, lemon zest

Blackberry-Bacon Grilled Cheese

This is a delicious sweet-and-spicy version (one of my favorite flavor combinations) of a traditional grilled cheese sandwich. Crisp bacon—another fave—adds a smoky element to the combo. This is excellent with my Cream of Tomato Soup on page 124.

SERVES 4   HANDS-ON 25 MINUTES   TOTAL 25 MINUTES

6 slices thick-cut bacon

2 tablespoons blackberry jam

2 teaspoons adobo sauce, from canned chipotle peppers in adobo sauce

4 tablespoons butter, softened

8 slices sourdough bread

4 slices Havarti cheese

¼ cup pickled jalapeño slices

1. Cook the bacon in a large skillet over medium-high 8 to 9 minutes or until crisp; remove the bacon, and drain on paper towels.

2. Stir together the blackberry jam and adobo sauce. Spread the butter on 1 side of each bread slice. Place 4 bread slices, buttered sides down, on wax paper. Top with the blackberry jam mixture, cheese, bacon, and pickled jalapeño peppers; top with the remaining bread slices, buttered sides up.

3. Cook the sandwiches in a nonstick skillet or preheated panini press over medium 2 to 3 minutes on each side or until golden brown and the cheese is melted.

AD LIB

You can change this up and experiment with it as much as you want. Use a different kind of cheese: Monterey Jack, Swiss . . . or pepper Jack, if you want it even spicier. I sometimes use raw jalapeños instead of the pickled kind for a bit of crunch and freshness. Shredded ham instead of bacon would be another good swap to turn this into a sweet-and-smoky, hot ham-and-cheese sandwich.

BLTA Chicken Salad

I love BLTA sandwiches—just a BLT with the addition of avocado. I also love grilled chicken, so combining these two flavors in a twist on chicken salad seemed like the best of both worlds! This is super fresh. I often serve it in lettuce wraps, but it's delicious sandwich-style as well. It can be served right after you make it, but I often make it a day ahead to let the flavors really meld.

SERVES 4 TO 6   HANDS-ON 30 MINUTES   TOTAL 30 MINUTES

1. Heat a grill pan over medium-high. Season the chicken breasts with the salt and pepper; rub with the olive oil. Cook the chicken 5 to 6 minutes on each side or until done. Let cool slightly, and then finely chop.

2. Whisk together the yogurt, mayonnaise, and lemon juice in a large bowl. Stir in the green onions, parsley, bacon, tomatoes, celery, and chopped cooked chicken. Season to taste with salt and pepper. Gently fold in the diced avocado. Serve over 6 cups chopped romaine lettuce or in 6 whole romaine leaves for a lettuce wrap.

AD LIB

I love tarragon. If you do too, add a little chopped tarragon to this mix. It's delicious with chicken.

3 medium boneless, skinless chicken breast halves (about 1¼ pounds)

½ teaspoon kosher salt

¼ teaspoon black pepper

2 teaspoons olive oil

½ cup plain Greek yogurt

¼ cup mayonnaise

2 teaspoons fresh lemon juice

1 green onion, chopped (about 2 tablespoons)

1 tablespoon chopped fresh parsley

6 slices thick-cut smoked bacon, cooked and chopped

1½ cups grape tomatoes, halved

1½ celery stalks, diced (½ cup)

1 ripe avocado, peeled and diced (about 1 cup)

6 romaine lettuce leaves (chopped or left whole)

Chicken Panini with Southwestern Pesto

Our whole family loves panini, especially Delaney. I mean what's not to love about delicious and delightful things pressed between two slices of bread? This is not a low-cal sandwich! Light mayo is an option if you are counting calories (but let's face it, if you are counting calories you are probably turning the page right now). If you want a yummy, rich, spicy, cheesy, toasted sandwich, this is one I highly recommend.

SERVES 4   HANDS-ON 30 MINUTES   TOTAL 30 MINUTES

SOUTHWESTERN PESTO

2 cups cilantro leaves and
   tender stems, packed

4 garlic cloves, chopped

1 jalapeño, seeded and
   chopped

Juice of ½ lime (about
   1½ tablespoons)

Pinch of kosher salt

2 tablespoons extra-virgin
   olive oil

CHIPOTLE MAYONNAISE

3 canned chipotle peppers in
   adobo sauce (2 tablespoons)

½ cup mayonnaise

1 teaspoon sugar

CHICKEN PANINI

3 tablespoons butter, softened

8 (½-inch-thick) sourdough
   bread slices

8 slices pepper Jack or Havarti
   cheese

6 ounces shredded rotisserie
   chicken or chopped cooked
   chicken (about 2 cups)

1. Prepare the Southwestern Pesto: Pulse the cilantro, garlic, jalapeño, lime juice, and salt in a food processor, fitted with the metal blade, 12 to 15 times or until finely chopped. With the machine running, slowly add the oil through the feed tube and process until a paste forms. Scrape the pesto into a small bowl. Set aside.

2. Prepare the Chipotle Mayo: Mince the chipotle peppers and add a bit of the adobo sauce, as needed, to measure 2 tablespoons. Stir together the mayonnaise, chipotles, and sugar in a small bowl.

3. Prepare the Panini: Spread the butter on 1 side of each bread slice. Turn the slices over, buttered sides down. Spread 4 bread slices with the chipotle mayonnaise and the other 4 bread slices with the cilantro pesto. Top 4 of the slices with the cheese and chicken, and top with the remaining bread slices, buttered sides up.

4. Cook the sandwiches in a large nonstick skillet (or griddle or panini press) over medium 2 to 3 minutes on each side or until golden brown and the cheese is melted.

AD LIB

If you want a spicier version, add more chipotle peppers to the mayo or don't seed the jalapeño for the pesto. Less spicy, less chipotle, and less jalapeño. If you have any leftover pesto, use it to top grilled chicken or add a little olive oil and you have a tasty marinade for shrimp.

Spicy Shrimp Po' Boys

John loves po'boys. Whenever we are touring the Gulf Coast, we search for the best local versions we can find. When we are in New Orleans, we make it our mission to eat all the traditional Cajun dishes: red beans and rice, jambalaya, and of course, dressed po'boys. I like mine spicy. Beware, this version has a kick. If you're making these for kids or for someone not quite as keen on spicy food, omit the cayenne. Use tail-off, peeled and deveined raw shrimp for this recipe.

SERVES 6   HANDS-ON 55 MINUTES   TOTAL 55 MINUTES

1. Stir together 2 tablespoons of the mustard, the mayonnaise, 2 teaspoons of the garlic powder, and 1 teaspoon of the cayenne in a small bowl. Set aside.

2. Whisk together the remaining ½ cup mustard and ½ cup water in a medium bowl. Add the shrimp, tossing to coat.

3. Whisk together the flour, cornmeal, salt, remaining 2 teaspoons garlic powder, and 1 teaspoon cayenne pepper in a medium bowl. Add the shrimp, and toss to coat.

4. Heat the oil to 375°F in a Dutch oven. Cook the shrimp 2 to 3 minutes per side or until golden. Drain on a wire rack set over a rimmed baking sheet lined with paper towels.

5. Preheat the broiler. Place the bread, cut sides up, on a baking sheet. Broil 8 inches from heat 1 minute to toast.

6. To assemble, spread the reserved mayonnaise mixture on the cut side of each roll. Add the fried shrimp, lettuce, and tomato slices. Serve warm.

TIP: To shred iceberg lettuce, separate and stack the leaves. Roll the stack up tightly (think fruit rollup), and slice thinly. If the pieces are too long, just cut them in half.

½ cup plus 2 tablespoons yellow mustard

½ cup mayonnaise

1 tablespoon plus 1 teaspoon garlic powder

2 teaspoons cayenne pepper

½ cup water

1½ pounds large shrimp, halved lengthwise

1 cup all-purpose flour

1 cup plain yellow cornmeal

2 teaspoons kosher salt

2 cups peanut or canola oil

6 (6-inch) French rolls, cut in half lengthwise

1 small head iceberg lettuce, thinly sliced (2 cups)

2 large tomatoes, thinly sliced

AD LIB

Make a Beef Po'boy with leftover Pot Roast with Gravy from page 173. Spread the toasted rolls with the mayo mixture, top with thinly sliced beef and a bit of gravy, and then top with the lettuce and tomato. Divine!

MARTINA'S KITCHEN MIX

MAIN
COURSES

I BELIEVE THAT FOOD IS MORE THAN JUST SUSTENANCE. Through sight, taste, and aroma, it can transport you right back to another place and time thanks to the memories associated with it. In this chapter, I've included new recipes and several old favorites. If I had to choose one dish from my childhood I remember best it would definitely be the Pot Roast with Gravy (page 173). My mom made it all the time. Now I make it mostly for special occasions. Food plays such a big part in memory and the smell of this pot roast cooking always takes me right back to our tiny farmhouse kitchen in Kansas, where I'm doing my homework or folding laundry, knowing that my mom was at the stove finishing up the gravy or whipping the creamy mashed potatoes. Since I save the dish for holidays, homecomings, birthdays, and times my family just needs a comforting meal, I know my girls will associate it with special times and memories of home too.

I'm always on the hunt for new recipes. I pore over cookbooks, magazines, and the Internet. (Ok, I'm a bit of a Pinterest addict!) I'm excited for you to try my spins on some of these new finds, like the Garlic-Roasted Cabbage "Steaks" with Eggplant-Tomato Sauce (page 158). I love experimenting with and adapting recipes to suit my tastes. The cabbage dish is a combination of a couple of recipes I found. You can serve it as a cabbage "steak" or break it apart so that it feels more like cabbage "pasta." Pretty cool! I also include a few favorite comfort foods from different parts of the world in this chapter. While I'm definitely not an expert on world cuisine, I must say that the recipe for Slow-Cooker Chicken Tikka Masala (page 169) is legit, and Julia Child's Eggplant Pizzas (page 153), enjoyed with a glass of red wine and a slice of fresh garlic bread, make me feel like I'm sitting down to a family meal in an Italian kitchen. It's hard to beat the fresh flavors of the Greek Grilled Chicken, Cucumber-Tomato Salad, and Tzatziki Sauce (page 160). It's sure to become a regular in your weeknight rotation.

I love the idea of others creating special memories around the recipes in this chapter. My hope is that a few of these recipes might become favorites that your family associates with warm moments together and special occasions. Maybe they'll get handed down to your next generation too. Enjoy!

Risotto with Asparagus, Peas, and Basil

I love risotto. All the stirring makes it a bit labor-intensive to make, but it's totally worth it. The wine gives this a nice tang. Chardonnay or Sauvignon Blanc is a good choice for this recipe. Obviously this makes a great "main attraction" but also makes a delicious and rich side for any grilled meat.

SERVES 8   HANDS-ON 45 MINUTES   TOTAL 45 MINUTES

1 pound asparagus

3⅓ cups chicken broth

1½ tablespoons butter

1 shallot, finely chopped

1 garlic clove, minced

1¼ cups uncooked arborio rice

1⅔ cups dry white wine

¾ cup frozen green peas, thawed

⅔ cup chopped basil

1 cup grated Parmesan cheese

Kosher salt and black pepper

Garnishes: basil sprigs, pea shoots (optional)

1. Cut away about 1 inch from the tougher base of each asparagus spear and discard. Cut off the tips and reserve separately. Cut the remaining stalks of the asparagus into small pieces to equal about 1½ cups.

2. Simmer the broth in a small saucepan over medium. Heat the butter in a large saucepan or Dutch oven over medium, and sauté the shallot and garlic until soft, about 1 minute. Add the rice, and sauté until well coated, 1 to 2 minutes. Add the wine and cook, stirring, until absorbed, about 5 minutes.

3. Add 1 cup of the warm broth. Cook over medium-high, stirring almost constantly, until absorbed. Continue adding the broth, 1 cup at a time, stirring until most of the liquid has been absorbed each time, about 25 minutes total. The rice should be tender, but not mushy, with a creamy consistency.

4. Add the asparagus pieces and cook, stirring constantly, for 2 to 3 minutes until the asparagus is tender. Add the peas, basil, and asparagus tips and stir in, cooking 2 to 3 minutes.

5. Remove from the heat; stir in the Parmesan. Season to taste with salt and pepper. Garnish with basil sprigs and pea shoots, if desired.

 TIP: Be sure to use arborio rice. You can find it in the grocery store or online.

Julia Child's Eggplant Pizzas

I love everything about this recipe. It's such a great and low-carb alternative to pizza. It's also extremely versatile because it can be used as a first course, a main course, or a side dish! I first introduced this to my carb-loving husband when I was trying to cook healthier for our family and also wanted more ideas for vegetarian dishes. I could tell he was skeptical at first but now it's one of his favorites! And I always feel good about making and serving it. As Julia would say, "Bon appétit!" (or, I guess in this case, "Buon appetito!").

SERVES 6   HANDS-ON 25 MINUTES   TOTAL 1 HOUR, 30 MINUTES

1. Preheat the oven to 375°F.

2. Sprinkle both sides of the eggplant slices generously with salt. Place in a single layer on paper towels lining a large rimmed baking sheet; let stand 30 minutes to allow slices to release moisture.

3. Heat 1 tablespoon of the olive oil in a large saucepan over medium. Add the onion, and cook, stirring occasionally, until tender, 5 to 7 minutes. Add the garlic and 1 teaspoon of the Italian seasoning, and cook 1 more minute. Add the tomatoes, red pepper, butter, and sugar, if desired. Cook over medium-low, stirring occasionally with a wooden spoon, about 30 minutes. Let cool slightly.

4. Wipe the eggplant slices to remove excess salt. Discard the paper towels and lightly grease the baking sheet. Brush the eggplant with the remaining 2 tablespoons olive oil. Sprinkle with the remaining 1 teaspoon Italian seasoning. Bake 20 minutes or until done but not mushy. Carefully remove the baking sheet from the oven using oven mitts.

5. Preheat the broiler.

6. Spread the tomato sauce evenly over the eggplant slices. Top evenly with the Parmesan and mozzarella. Return the baking sheet to the oven and broil 6 inches from the heat for 3 to 4 minutes or just until the cheese is melted. Sprinkle with the basil and additional red pepper, if desired.

1 large eggplant, sliced into ½-inch rounds (about 1½ pounds)

Kosher salt

3 tablespoons olive oil

1 small sweet onion, diced (about ½ cup)

2 garlic cloves, minced

2 teaspoons dried Italian seasoning

1 (28-ounce) can crushed tomatoes

¼ teaspoon crushed red pepper, plus more for sprinkling

3 tablespoons butter

1½ teaspoons sugar (optional)

⅓ cup grated Parmesan cheese

1 cup grated mozzarella cheese

1 tablespoon chopped fresh basil (optional)

Chicken and Potatoes with Roasted Lemon and Rosemary Sauce

This is inspired by a recipe from one of my all-time favorite restaurants, Tra Vigne, in Napa. We often end up with a day off in Napa during the summer when we tour the West Coast. One tradition was to end the day with a fantastic meal on the patio at Tra Vigne. They had a railroad track that ran behind the restaurant, and when the girls were little, John put pennies on the track with them. They loved it when the train came by and were amazed when they saw their flattened pennies. Tra Vigne is closed now. It was the end of an era for us, but this dish reminds me of the happy times spent there surrounded by string lights, flickering candles, and great wine, with my family, band, and crew sharing stories and laughing until we closed the place down.

SERVES 4 TO 6   HANDS-ON 40 MINUTES   TOTAL 40 MINUTES

1½ pounds small new potatoes

2 large lemons

¼ cup olive oil plus more for brushing on lemons

Kosher salt and freshly ground black pepper

4 boneless chicken breast halves, skin on (leaving the skin on is optional)

2 tablespoons minced garlic

2 cups chicken broth

1 teaspoon finely chopped fresh rosemary

1 tablespoon finely chopped fresh flat-leaf parsley

1 tablespoon unsalted butter

1. Bring the potatoes and water to cover to a boil in a large Dutch oven over medium-high, and cook 10 minutes or just until tender. Drain. Let cool slightly; cut the potatoes in half.

2. Preheat the broiler. Cut the lemons in half. Arrange, flesh side up, in a flameproof, nonreactive baking dish. Brush with olive oil, and season with salt and pepper. Broil 6 inches or more from the heat until browned and soft, about 6 to 10 minutes. Let cool.

3. Squeeze the lemon halves over a fine mesh strainer set over a bowl. Push and stir the pulp through the strainer with a rubber spatula or wooden spoon. Discard the lemon shells. Set aside the roasted lemon juice.

4. Preheat the oven to 450°F. Season the chicken with the salt and pepper. Heat the remaining ¼ cup olive oil in a large ovenproof sauté pan over medium-high until hot. Add the chicken, and cook 5 minutes on each side until almost cooked through. Remove to a platter.

5. Return the pan to medium-high, add the potatoes, and cook, stirring occasionally and tossing until browned all over, about 5 minutes. Arrange the chicken on top of the potatoes.

Bake 10 minutes or until the chicken is done; transfer the chicken to a platter. Cook the potatoes in the pan over medium-high, tossing well so the pan juices are absorbed into the potatoes, about 5 minutes. Arrange the potatoes around the chicken.

6. Return the pan to medium-high. Add the garlic and cook 30 seconds. Add the reserved roasted lemon juice, broth, rosemary, parsley, and butter, stirring to loosen the browned bits from the bottom of the pan. Cook 5 minutes, stirring occasionally. Season to taste with the salt and pepper. Pour the sauce over the chicken and potatoes, and serve immediately.

Cheese Tortellini with Gorgonzola Cream Sauce and Toasted Walnuts

---

This recipe will always be associated with a special memory for me. I was in the process of testing this dish for the book when we went to pick up Emma from the airport. It was her first visit home in several months after her move to Los Angeles. She was starving, so I served her a plate of this creamy pasta and she loved it. I was just so happy to have her back in my kitchen and to be cooking for her again. Who wouldn't love this pasta? The sauce is rich and full of flavor and it comes together quickly, which makes it perfect for a busy weeknight meal. At the same time, it's elegant enough to serve to company.

SERVES 4   HANDS-ON 30 MINUTES   TOTAL 30 MINUTES

1. Cook the cream, wine, and broth in a 3½-quart saucepan over medium for 20 minutes or until reduced by half (about 1 cup).

2. Whisk in the Gorgonzola and nutmeg until the sauce is smooth. Keep warm over low heat, stirring occasionally.

3. Cook the tortellini according to the package directions; drain and toss the hot pasta with the Gorgonzola cream sauce. Top with the walnuts and a few fresh parsley leaves, if desired, just before serving.

1 cup heavy cream

½ cup dry white wine

½ cup chicken broth

4 ounces Gorgonzola cheese

Generous pinch of ground nutmeg

1 (20-ounce) package refrigerated cheese-filled tortellini or ravioli

½ cup chopped toasted walnuts (see page 106)

Garnish: fresh parsley leaves

Garlic-Roasted Cabbage "Steaks" with Eggplant-Tomato Sauce

I discovered the idea of adding eggplant to my sauce by accident. I was making marinara for pasta and had a little eggplant leftover so I just chopped it up and added it to the sauce. I liked the depth of flavor it added. The sauce is great on any type of pasta and zucchini noodles as well.

SERVES 4   **HANDS-ON 25 MINUTES**   **TOTAL 1 HOUR, 45 MINUTES, INCLUDING SAUCE**

1 (1½-pound) head of green cabbage

1½ tablespoons olive oil

2 large garlic cloves, crushed

½ teaspoon kosher salt

¼ teaspoon black pepper

Eggplant Tomato Sauce (recipe follows)

¼ cup feta cheese

1 (4.25-ounce) can chopped black olives, drained

2 tablespoons chopped fresh basil

1. Preheat the oven to 400°F. Wash the cabbage and slice into (4) 2-inch-thick slices.

2. Transfer to a lightly greased medium-size rimmed baking sheet. Brush both sides of the cabbage with the olive oil. Rub both sides of the cabbage slices with the garlic, tucking garlic into the crevices of the cabbage slices, and sprinkle with the salt and pepper.

3. Bake for 45 minutes or until the edges are crispy, turning after 20 minutes.

4. Top with the Eggplant Tomato Sauce, feta cheese, olives, and basil.

Eggplant-Tomato Sauce

1 tablespoon olive oil

1 medium onion, chopped (about ¾ cup)

½ cup finely chopped eggplant

2 garlic cloves, minced

1 teaspoon smoked paprika

1 (14.5-ounce) can crushed fire-roasted tomatoes

½ teaspoon kosher salt

¼ teaspoon black pepper

1 teaspoon sugar

Heat the oil in a medium skillet over medium-high. Cook the onion and eggplant in the skillet 5 to 7 minutes or just until tender. Add the garlic and paprika, and cook for 2 minutes. Add the tomatoes, salt, and pepper, and simmer 25 to 30 minutes. Stir in the sugar. Makes 1¾ cups

AD LIB

For a low-carb version of a pasta-like dish, you can slice the cabbage a little thinner, cut the roasting time down to 30 to 35 minutes, and break up the cabbage so that you have cabbage "noodles." Toss them with the sauce, then top with the feta and olives.

Greek Grilled Chicken, Cucumber-Tomato Salad, and Tzatziki Sauce

---

This is my go-to chicken recipe because it's so versatile, plus John and our girls love it! I grill it in a grill pan and use it regularly on a big ol' salad of romaine, broccoli and cauliflower florets, green pepper, tomatoes, cucumbers—whatever I find in the fridge—and top it with a simple dressing made up of olive oil, lemon juice, and salt and pepper to taste. It's delicious and so healthy!

Combined with Tzatziki Sauce and Cucumber-Tomato Salad, this Greek Chicken is an ideal lunch bowl. I've started prepping lunch bowls and making a few at a time to enjoy throughout the week. It makes a healthy lunch so easy when it's all made up and in the fridge ready to grab.

SERVES 4   HANDS-ON 1 HOUR
TOTAL 2 HOURS, 45 MINUTES, INCLUDING SALAD, SAUCE, AND MARINATING

4 boneless, skinless chicken breasts

½ teaspoon poultry seasoning (optional)

½ teaspoon kosher salt

¼ teaspoon black pepper

⅓ cup fresh lemon juice plus juice of 1 lemon

3 tablespoons minced garlic

1 tablespoon chopped fresh oregano

1 tablespoon chopped fresh rosemary

¼ cup olive oil

⅓ cup plain Greek yogurt

Pinch of crushed red pepper (optional)

Cucumber-Tomato Salad (recipe follows)

Tzatziki Sauce (recipe follows)

1. Season the chicken with the poultry seasoning, if desired, and the salt and pepper. In a large ziplock plastic bag, combine ⅓ cup of the lemon juice, minced garlic, oregano, rosemary, olive oil, yogurt, and crushed red pepper, if desired. Add the chicken to the bag and massage it to make sure the chicken is fully coated. Marinate in the refrigerator at least 30 minutes or up to 12 hours, turning occasionally.

2. Preheat a grill to medium (about 350° to 400°F).

3. Remove the chicken from the marinade, discarding the marinade. Let the chicken stand at room temperature for 30 minutes.

4. Grill the chicken, covered, 10 to 12 minutes, turning once. Remove from the heat, and let stand 10 minutes.

5. Slice the chicken on the diagonal; squeeze the juice of the remaining lemon over the chicken. Serve with the Cucumber-Tomato Salad and Tzatziki Sauce.

Cucumber-Tomato Salad

½ English cucumber, peeled, seeded, and diced (about 1 cup)

1 cup seeded diced tomatoes or halved grape or cherry tomatoes

1 green bell pepper, chopped (about 1 cup)

½ small red onion, chopped (about ¼ cup)

¼ cup chopped fresh flat-leaf parsley

¼ cup pepperoncini salad peppers

⅓ cup lime juice

1 tablespoon extra-virgin olive oil

1 tablespoon red wine vinegar

Stir together the cucumber, tomatoes, bell pepper, onion, parsley, peppers, lime juice, olive oil, and vinegar in a medium bowl; let stand at least 20 minutes. Makes about 4 cups

Tzatziki Sauce

½ English cucumber, peeled and grated

1 cup plain Greek yogurt

½ cup crumbled Greek feta cheese

2 teaspoons chopped fresh dill

1 tablespoon chopped fresh flat-leaf parsley

1 garlic clove, grated

Juice of ½ lemon

1. Salt the grated cucumber, and drain in a colander for 30 minutes.

2. Press out as much liquid as you can, and transfer to a food processor.

3. Add the yogurt, feta, dill, parsley, garlic, and lemon juice, and process until smooth, about 20 seconds.

4. Season to taste with salt and black pepper. Cover and refrigerate until ready to use. Makes 1½ cups

AD LIB

You can also serve this in a pita. Just put the chicken and salad and sauce right in there! Add in a little brown rice for texture and filling fiber, if you wish.

Stuffed Poblano Peppers with Lime Crema

I made this the first time when my longtime lead guitar player brought me fresh poblanos from his garden. Since it makes enough filling to stuff about 8 peppers, it's great for a dinner party. These are terrific warmed up the next day for lunch. Freeze any leftover filling for later use. Dried currants (often sold as Zante currants) can be hard to find. They add a bit of welcome sweetness to the filling.

SERVES 6 TO 8   HANDS-ON 45 MINUTES
TOTAL 1 HOUR, 15 MINUTES, INCLUDING SAUCE

8 poblano peppers
¾ cup uncooked long-grain white rice or cauliflower rice
1 pound lean ground beef
1 yellow onion, diced (about 1 cup)
6 garlic cloves, minced
½ teaspoon kosher salt
¼ teaspoon black pepper
4 tablespoons tomato paste
4 teaspoons ground cumin
¼ cup dried currants (finely chopped dates or chopped dried cranberries may be substituted)
Lime Crema (recipe follows)

1. Preheat the broiler.

2. Place the poblanos on a foil-lined rimmed baking sheet. Broil 3 inches from the heat for 7 to 8 minutes, or until blackened, turning after 3 to 4 minutes. Place in a paper bag or a large ziplock plastic bag; fold to close tightly. Let steam 15 minutes to loosen skins. Peel and discard the skins. When the peppers are cool enough to handle, cut a lengthwise slit in each pepper without going all the way through. Remove the seeds and membranes. Set the peppers aside.

3. Preheat the oven to 350°F. Cook the rice according to the package directions.

4. While the peppers steam, add the beef, onion, and garlic to a large skillet over medium-high. Cook, stirring frequently, until the meat crumbles and is no longer pink, 8 to 10 minutes. Drain off any excess grease. Season the meat with the salt and pepper. Stir in the tomato paste, cumin, rice, and currants, and cook 2 to 3 minutes until fragrant and warmed through.

5. Fill each pepper with the beef mixture. Return the stuffed peppers to the baking sheet and bake 5 minutes. Serve topped with the Lime Crema.

AD LIB

This filling would be just as good (and less spicy) in bell peppers or zucchini boats. Top with mozzarella cheese instead of the Lime Crema.

Lime Crema

½ cup sour cream (plain Greek yogurt
   may be substituted)

2 teaspoons fresh lime juice

1 tablespoon chopped fresh cilantro

Whisk together the sour cream, lime juice, and cilantro in a small bowl. Season to taste with salt and black pepper. Makes about ½ cup

Chili Lime Chicken Tacos with Grilled Pineapple Salsa and Avocado Crema

This recipe takes a little work, but it's so worth it! It's loaded with some of my favorite go-to basic recipes, and the versatility is definitely impressive. Tacos are trendy and this particular recipe hits all the right notes.

SERVES 6   HANDS-ON 20 MINUTES   TOTAL 2 HOURS, 20 MINUTES

1. Combine the chicken and Southwest Citrus Rub in a ziplock freezer bag.

2. Chill at least 2 hours and up to 6 hours.

3. Preheat a grill to medium-high (about 450°F).

4. Remove the chicken from the bag with the rub; grill 5 minutes on each side or until done. Slice the chicken and serve in the flour tortillas with the Grilled Pineapple Salsa, Avocado Crema, and grated pepper Jack cheese.

2 pounds boneless, skinless chicken breasts
Southwest Citrus Rub (page 248)
12 to 18 (6-inch) flour tortillas, warmed
Grilled Pineapple Salsa (page 251)
Avocado Crema (page 251)
Grated pepper Jack cheese

AD LIB

Grilled pork tenderloin would be delicious here with the sweet pineapple and the citrus rub.

Chicken Braised in Sun-Dried Tomato Cream Sauce

———

This is a recipe I have made again and again for several years. As a matter of fact, this was in my first "cookbook" (a little book I printed for friends and family). It's so quick and easy. One of my friends makes it all the time and his family calls it "Martina's Chicken." Using the oil straight from the jar of sun-dried tomatoes gives the chicken lots of flavor.

SERVES 4 TO 6   HANDS-ON 20 MINUTES   TOTAL 20 MINUTES

4 chicken breast cutlets (about 1 pound)

½ teaspoon kosher salt

¼ teaspoon black pepper

¼ cup thinly sliced sun-dried tomatoes in oil, plus 1 tablespoon oil from the jar

3 garlic cloves, thinly sliced

½ cup dry white wine

½ cup heavy cream

3 tablespoons thinly sliced basil leaves

Garnish: basil sprigs

1. Pat the chicken dry. Season with the salt and pepper. Heat 1 tablespoon oil from the jar in a large skillet over medium-high. Cook the chicken 1 minute on each side or just until golden.

2. Remove the chicken. Stir in the garlic; cook 30 seconds. Add the wine, cream, and tomatoes, stirring to scrape the brown bits from the bottom of the skillet. Cook over medium-high until the mixture comes to a boil. Add the chicken, and reduce the heat to medium-low.

3. Cover and cook 5 minutes or just until the chicken is done. Transfer the chicken to a serving plate, and add the basil to the sauce. Season to taste with the salt and pepper, and serve over the chicken. Top with the thinly sliced basil. Garnish with basil sprigs, if desired.

AD LIB

Serve this with a green vegetable, garlic, and mashed potatoes . . . or turn it into a super-quick, one-pot chicken and pasta dish. My family loves it this way. Just cook ¼ pound angel hair pasta. After the chicken is cooked in the sauce, cut it into bite-size pieces. Add the basil and pasta to the sauce and stir until the pasta is coated. Return the chicken to the pan and toss it with the pasta and sauce. Add a green salad and you have a complete dinner on the table in about 20 minutes!

Slow-Cooker Chicken Tikka Masala

One of the best meals I've had was with my band and crew at Bombay Brasserie in London. None of us knew much about Indian cuisine so we let the chef send out whatever he wanted. All the exotic flavors and aromas (and the flowing wine) made for a fabulous culinary adventure that we still talk about today. Chicken Tikka Masala is a favorite Indian dish of mine, so I was excited to learn to make an authentic version at home. This recipe may seem daunting, but it is actually simple to make. Serve this with naan, an Indian flatbread. (I buy it from a local Indian restaurant or grocery store.)

SERVES 6 TO 8   HANDS-ON 30 MINUTES
TOTAL 5 HOURS, 30 MINUTES, INCLUDING 1 HOUR CHILLING

1. Stir together the yogurt, lemon juice, 2 teaspoons of the cumin, cayenne, cinnamon, salt, and pepper in a large bowl. Add the chicken; toss to coat completely with the marinade. Cover and place in the fridge at least 1 hour or overnight.

2. Preheat the broiler. Place the chicken on a lightly greased rack in a foil-lined broiler pan. Broil 5 inches from the heat for 5 minutes on each side.

3. Heat the oil in a skillet over medium-high. Add the onion, garlic, and ginger; sauté 1 minute. Transfer to a lightly greased 6-quart slow cooker. Stir in the diced tomatoes, tomato paste, 3 teaspoons of the garam masala, tikka paste, 1 teaspoon of the cumin, 1 teaspoon of the chili powder, and coriander. Cut the broiled chicken into 2-inch pieces. Add to the slow cooker, and stir to combine. Cover; cook on HIGH 4 to 6 hours.

4. Before serving, stir in the remaining ½ teaspoon garam masala, ½ teaspoon cumin, and ½ teaspoon chili powder. Season with salt. Stir in the cream and fresh cilantro. Serve over rice.

variation

Vegetarian Tikka Masala: Substitute 1½ cups uncooked red lentils for the chicken, omitting marinating in yogurt and spices. Proceed with the recipe as directed, cooking on HIGH for 3 to 4 hours or LOW for 5 to 6 hours.

1 cup plain yogurt

1 tablespoon lemon juice

3½ teaspoons ground cumin

¼ to 1 teaspoon cayenne pepper

1 teaspoon ground cinnamon

1 teaspoon kosher salt

1 teaspoon black pepper

6 boneless, skinless chicken breasts (about 4 pounds)

1 tablespoon vegetable oil

1 medium onion, diced (1 cup)

2 garlic cloves, minced

1 tablespoon grated fresh ginger

1 (28-ounce) can diced tomatoes, undrained

1 (6-ounce) can tomato paste

3½ teaspoons garam masala

1 tablespoon tikka paste

1½ teaspoons chili powder

1 teaspoon dried coriander

1 cup heavy cream

2 tablespoons chopped fresh cilantro

6 cups cooked basmati rice

Pot Roast with Gravy

This recipe is my mom's specialty. She handed this recipe and method down to each of her kids. It tastes like home to me, and I make it for all the holidays in our house. I love how it fills my whole house with its delicious aroma! Sometimes I open the door and walk outside for a minute just so I can come back in and smell it! I love the idea that one day I will teach my girls how to make this recipe and that they will be re-creating it in their own homes.

SERVES 8   HANDS-ON 25 MINUTES   TOTAL 3 HOURS, 55 MINUTES

1. Season the roast with the salt and pepper. Rub the entire roast with the garlic, tucking into the roast's nooks and crannies as you go.

2. Heat the oil in a large Dutch oven over medium-high. Sear the roast 4 minutes on each side or until browned all over. (This is key to great flavor!) Pour the beef broth over the roast and top with alternating slices of onion and green bell pepper to cover the top of the roast. Cover and cook over low until the meat is tender, about 3½ hours.

3. Discard the onion and green pepper slices. Remove the cooked roast to a serving platter. Reserve ½ cup pan juices; whisk in the cornstarch until smooth. Heat the juices remaining in the pan over medium-high. Slowly whisk in the cornstarch mixture and cook over medium-high, whisking constantly, until slightly thickened, about 5 minutes. Slice the roast, and serve with the pan gravy.

TIP: I go back and forth between using flour and using cornstarch for the gravy. I have done both. If you decide to use flour, or you have no cornstarch on hand, make a slurry with the flour and a mixture of warm water (not too hot) and a bit of the cooking juices, slightly cooled. Pour this mixture slowly into the liquid in the pan and bring to a boil, whisking constantly, until thickened. Serve this gravy over mashed potatoes for a little piece of heaven.

1 (4-pound) chuck roast
1½ teaspoons kosher salt
½ teaspoon black pepper
3 garlic cloves, minced
2 tablespoons vegetable oil
2½ cups beef broth
3 onion slices
3 green bell pepper slices
2 tablespoons cornstarch

Pan-Roasted Halibut

Fresh, simple ingredients make up this recipe. Up until about a year ago, I was really intimidated by the thought of cooking fish. I just never did it. But I finally jumped in and realized how easy it is to prepare. My favorite fish is mild, white fish, like halibut and grouper, with no "fishy" taste. Either would work here. In this recipe, we first sear the fish in a pan on the stovetop over high heat to create a crust, and then finish it in the oven. So easy! If you're making dinner for two, just prepare two fillets instead of four. And if you don't like spinach, use green beans, asparagus—or really anything green and fresh that looks pretty on the plate. (Although I wouldn't turn down a side of creamy risotto or even creamed spinach instead of sautéed with this. Balance, right?) The Pesto Butter adds a lot of flavor but can be omitted.

SERVES 4   HANDS-ON 20 MINUTES   TOTAL 30 MINUTES

4 (6-ounce) halibut fillets

3 tablespoons unsalted butter, melted

1 teaspoon kosher salt

½ teaspoon black pepper

1½ to 2 cups panko (Japanese breadcrumbs)

2 tablespoons olive oil

1 cup halved grape tomatoes

Pesto Butter (page 259)

Sautéed Spinach (page 197)

1. Preheat the oven to 425°F.

2. Brush the halibut with the melted butter, and season with the salt and pepper. Coat the fish evenly with the breadcrumbs, pressing to adhere.

3. Cook the fish in the hot oil in a large ovenproof skillet over medium-high 3 minutes. Turn the fish, and add the tomatoes to the pan. Bake the fish for 10 minutes or just until the fish flakes with a fork.

4. Top each fillet with 1 tablespoon of room temperature Pesto Butter, and serve with Sautéed Spinach.

Pesto Butter Tip: You will have butter left over. Just pop it in the fridge or freezer and remember to use it next time you make a chicken panini. It's also a great and easy way to liven up plain pasta. It will keep in the fridge 2 weeks and up to 3 months tightly wrapped in the freezer.

Blackened Fish Taco Bowls

—

I made this for the first time in the summer for a lunch with friends by the pool. I feel like this is a healthy recipe and something that even people who aren't that into fish will love. It's light and fresh, but satisfying. I like it warm or cold. And you can make it as mild or as spicy as you want by adjusting the amount of cayenne pepper. This is pretty layered in bowls, but my favorite way to serve it is to just mix it all up in a large bowl and serve as individual portions.

SERVES 4   HANDS-ON 30 MINUTES   TOTAL 40 MINUTES

1. Cook the rice according to the package directions, and keep warm.

2. Stir together the chili powder, cumin, salt, and cayenne in a small bowl. Rub evenly over the fish.

3. Heat a 10-inch cast-iron skillet over high just until the skillet begins to smoke. Remove it from the heat and add 2 teaspoons of the canola oil and the fish. Return to the stove and reduce the heat to medium-high. Cook 3 minutes. Turn the fish and cook until done, about 4 minutes more.

4. Remove the fish from the skillet, flake into 1-inch pieces, and keep warm. Add the remaining 1 teaspoon canola oil to the skillet, and stir in the garlic, green onions, red bell pepper, and corn. Cook 2 to 3 minutes or until the corn is golden brown, stirring frequently. Stir in the beans, and cook 1 minute.

5. Layer the rice in the bottom of 4 individual bowls or 1 large serving bowl. Top with the corn and bean mixture, fish, and avocado. Drizzle with the lime juice, and top with the fresh cilantro. Garnish, if desired.

AD LIB

Substitute 3 cups cooked quinoa for the brown rice. Proceed with the recipe as directed.

1 cup uncooked brown rice

1 tablespoon chili powder

1 teaspoon ground cumin

½ teaspoon kosher salt

¼ to ½ teaspoon cayenne pepper

2 (8-ounce) mild white fish fillets (such as grouper or halibut)

3 teaspoons canola oil

2 garlic cloves, minced

2 green onions, sliced (about ¼ cup)

1 red bell pepper, chopped (about 1 cup)

1 cup fresh corn kernels (2 ears)

1 cup canned black beans, drained and rinsed

½ large avocado, diced (about ½ cup)

Juice from 1 lime (about 2 tablespoons)

¼ cup chopped fresh cilantro

Garnishes: lime wedges, cilantro sprigs

Slow-Roasted Garlic-Dijon Salmon

———

One of the things I'm most proud of is that I've started cooking fish regularly for our family. This salmon recipe is perfect for a novice cook. It's basically foolproof. Slow-roasting salmon somehow tames any strong "fishy" flavors too. The result is just buttery, rich salmon. It's hard to overcook it using this method. This flavorful fish pairs beautifully with steamed broccoli and a simple salad. It's sooo healthy!!

SERVES 4   HANDS-ON 20 MINUTES   TOTAL 45 MINUTES

1 (1½-pound) salmon fillet

2 tablespoons chopped fresh flat-leaf parsley

3 garlic cloves, pressed

1½ teaspoons Dijon mustard

½ teaspoon kosher salt

¼ teaspoon black pepper

2 tablespoons olive oil

2 tablespoons fresh lemon juice

2 small lemons, sliced

1. Preheat the oven to 275°F.

2. Cut the salmon into 4 (6-ounce) portions.

3. Place the salmon, skin side down, on a rimmed baking sheet lined with lightly greased aluminum foil. Stir together the parsley, garlic, Dijon, salt, pepper, olive oil, and lemon juice in a small bowl. Spoon the mixture over the salmon, and arrange the lemon slices over the top.

4. Bake 25 to 30 minutes until the fish is just opaque all the way through.

TIP: I like my fish cooked more well-done. Growing up in Kansas I was basically not exposed to fresh seafood, so well-done is just a comfort level thing for me. As a rule of thumb, the fish should flake when you break into it with a fork, but still be moist.

I've also learned to remove the cooked skin from the bottom after it cooks. It turns into basically a very thin layer that you can scrape off with a knife. It really helps eliminate any "fishy" taste.

If you need to get dinner on the table quickly, you can roast the salmon at 450°F for 12 to 15 minutes.

Grilled Shrimp Tacos

Until a few years ago, I'd made only ground beef tacos. Now, it seems, everything turns up in a taco. These shrimp tacos are healthy, delicious, and simple to prepare.

**SERVES 8   HANDS-ON 45 MINUTES
TOTAL 45 MINUTES, INCLUDING SLAW AND SAUCE**

1. Preheat a grill to medium-high (about 450°F) or use a grill pan. Coat a cold cooking grate with cooking spray, and place on the grill.

2. Whisk together the lime juice, olive oil, chili powder, and salt in a medium bowl; add the shrimp, tossing to coat.

3. Grill the shrimp, uncovered, 3 to 4 minutes on each side or just until the shrimp turn pink.

4. Fill the warmed flour tortillas with the shrimp and Red Slaw, and drizzle with the Chipotle Sauce.

½ cup lime juice (from about 4 limes)

1 tablespoon olive oil

2 teaspoons chili powder

1 teaspoon kosher salt

2 pounds raw large shrimp, peeled and deveined

16 to 20 (6-inch) flour tortillas, warmed

Red Slaw (recipe follows)

Chipotle Sauce (page 259)

Red Slaw

1 tablespoon extra-virgin olive oil

1 tablespoon white vinegar

4 cups shredded red cabbage (½ medium cabbage)

½ cup chopped green onions (about 4 green onions)

½ cup chopped fresh cilantro

Whisk together the olive oil and vinegar in a medium bowl. Stir in the cabbage, green onions, and cilantro. Season to taste with salt and black pepper. Makes about 4 cups

AD LIB

This recipe is just as good with a mild white fish such as halibut or grouper. The Chipotle Sauce is very versatile and can be used in lots of ways—topping a baked potato, whipped into mashed potatoes, as a dip for shrimp cocktail, or as a spread for a sandwich to add a little kick. Or try adding the Red Slaw to a pulled pork sandwich and top with barbecue sauce and sweet pickles.

MARTINA'S KITCHEN MIX

SIDE DISHES

ONCE YOU DECIDE what you are serving for the main course, it's time to figure out the accompaniments to complement and round out the meal. Think of the recipes in this chapter as accessories. The way the perfect pair of earrings or scarf can add just the right finishing touch to your outfit, these dishes can add the perfect accent to your meal. If you compare a meal to recording music, the main course is like the basic track. When I record a song in the studio, I get the basics first . . . drums, bass, guitar, and piano. That's the main focus. But oftentimes it's the extras we add . . . a string part, background vocals, or percussion, for example, that make you really fall in love with a record. In this way, I think of side dishes as the "overdubs" to the "basic track" of the main course.

I like interesting, creative side dishes and familiar, comfy ones too. I honestly think side dishes can make or break a meal. At a restaurant, my decision on what to order is often based on what comes with the entrée. (I've also been known to order only side dishes!) When I'm cooking, I consider sides as an opportunity to balance the meal through complementary flavors and textures, but also to boost nutrition. Most of the recipes here are vegetable-based so they add healthy interest to a plate.

These days it can be hard to keep track of dietary restrictions and trends when you have people over for dinner. With so many different diets in play now—Paleo, Keto, Vegan, Vegetarian—side dishes are even more important. I always offer several to give my guests choices so no one leaves feeling hungry. Some of the recipes here, like the Sautéed Kale with Parmesan and Toasted Walnuts (page 200) and the Roasted Cinnamon "Harrisburgs" (aka Brussels Sprouts) (page 207), can easily double as vegetarian main courses. Roast up a pan of either the Roasted Summer Veggies or Spicy Roasted Fall Veggies (pages 193 and 194) for a guaranteed crowd-pleaser. (I've been known to eat them as my whole meal, straight off the baking sheet!) Adding a side or two from this chapter to the entrées you serve will make a lasting impression on your satisfied guests.

Roasted Asparagus with Lemon, Parmesan, and Garlic

I love fresh asparagus. When I was a kid growing up in Kansas, we ate asparagus only from a can. Actually we ate most of our vegetables from a can . . . green beans, corn, peas, spinach. That may seem strange since we lived on a farm, but our garden was saved mostly for tomatoes. If you've never tasted a Kansas tomato, you're missing out! While I love asparagus cooked all kinds of ways, this roasted version with lemon and Parmesan really takes it up a notch. The bright green asparagus beneath a mound of fluffy Parmesan cheese makes this one gorgeous side dish.

SERVES 4 TO 6   HANDS-ON 10 MINUTES   TOTAL 18 MINUTES

1 pound asparagus, trimmed

2 tablespoons olive oil

½ teaspoon kosher salt

¼ teaspoon black pepper

2 garlic cloves, pressed

3 tablespoons grated Parmesan cheese

2 tablespoons fresh lemon juice

Garnish: lemon wedges

1. Preheat the oven to 400°F.

2. Toss the asparagus with the olive oil, salt, pepper, and garlic in a large bowl.

3. Arrange in a single layer on a lightly greased large rimmed baking sheet. Bake for 8 minutes or until the asparagus is tender-crisp.

4. Return to the bowl, and add the Parmesan and lemon juice, tossing to coat. Garnish with lemon wedges, if desired. Serve immediately.

TIP: The bottom ends of asparagus spears are often tough and fibrous unlike the tender tips. Trim away the bottom inch or two, or do what I do and bend the base of each spear and it will snap where the tender part begins, and you can discard the ends.

Smashed New Potatoes with Lemon

Lemon adds an unexpected twist to the traditional potato side dish. I especially like these in the spring and summer months and they are my go-to when dining al fresco. The trouble is . . . I cannot stop eating them!

SERVES 6   HANDS-ON 15 MINUTES   TOTAL 30 MINUTES

1. Arrange the potatoes in a steamer basket over boiling water. Cover and steam 15 to 20 minutes or until tender. Or cook in boiling water 15 minutes until tender.

2. Lightly smash the potatoes, toss with the oil and lemon zest, and season with salt and pepper.

3 pounds small red new potatoes

¼ cup extra-virgin olive oil

2 teaspoons lemon zest (from 1 lemon)

Kosher salt and freshly ground black pepper

Green Beans with Goat Cheese and Warm Bacon Dressing

What you have here, folks, is a real workhorse of a side dish. I've added this to a brunch menu, made it as a side dish for Thanksgiving, taken it to a potluck, and made it in each of the four seasons. If you haven't noticed, I love goat cheese and I love dried cranberries (as evidenced by the many uses of those two ingredients in this book), but if your life is dairy-free, these beans are just as delicious without the goat cheese.

SERVES 12   HANDS-ON 45 MINUTES   TOTAL 30 MINUTES

3 pounds green beans, trimmed

½ pound smoked bacon, chopped (about 6 to 8 slices)

½ cup chopped shallots (about 3)

2 garlic cloves, chopped

¼ cup sherry wine vinegar

3 tablespoons Dijon mustard

1 teaspoon dry mustard

½ cup extra-virgin olive oil

Kosher salt and freshly ground black pepper

1 cup crumbled goat cheese

½ cup dried sweetened cranberries

1. Cook the beans in a large pot of boiling water until tender-crisp, about 5 minutes. Drain.

2. Rinse with cold water, and drain. Pat dry. (Beans can be prepared 1 day ahead. Wrap in paper towels, put in a ziplock plastic bag, and chill. Bring to room temp before continuing.)

3. Place the beans in a large bowl. Cook the bacon in a skillet, and transfer to paper towels to drain, reserving the drippings in skillet. Add the shallots and garlic to the drippings in skillet. Sauté over medium, 1 minute or just until soft. Add the vinegar, Dijon, and dry mustard. Whisk, stirring to loosen the browned bits in the bottom of the skillet. Whisk in the olive oil. Season with salt and black pepper.

4. Toss the beans with the warm dressing. Sprinkle with the bacon, goat cheese and dried cranberries. Serve immediately.

Roasted Summer Veggies with Herbs

I love to roast vegetables any time of year. They are so good for you. I make a big batch and just use them in lunches and as side dishes during the week. Feel free to add or subtract your preferred vegetables, and obviously this recipe can be halved for fewer servings. These would be great drizzled with the Green Goddess Dressing (page 255).

SERVES 10 TO 12   HANDS-ON 25 MINUTES   TOTAL 45 MINUTES

1. Preheat the oven to 400°F.

2. Stir together the sweet potatoes, new potatoes, cauliflower, onion, tomatoes, garlic, rosemary, thyme, olive oil, salt, and pepper in a large bowl. Transfer to 2 lightly greased large rimmed baking sheets. Bake anywhere from 20-30 minutes, until golden brown or slightly charred, rotating the pans and stirring halfway through. Add the asparagus to the baking sheet during the last 15 minutes of cooking to cook until tender and the vegetables are golden brown.

2 large sweet potatoes, peeled and cut into ¾-inch cubes (about 2 pounds)

1 pound new potatoes, halved

1½ pounds cauliflower, cut into large florets

1 sweet onion, cut into eighths

1 pint cherry tomatoes

3 garlic cloves, peeled and halved

1 teaspoon chopped fresh rosemary

½ teaspoon chopped fresh thyme

2 tablespoons olive oil

1 teaspoon kosher salt

½ teaspoon black pepper

1 pound asparagus, trimmed and cut into 1-inch pieces

Spicy Roasted Fall Veggies with Herbs

I have made roasted vegetables so many times that one day I was looking for a way to change them up a little. So I just started adding spices and things to give them a kick. You can control the spiciness by reducing or eliminating (or increasing 'cause that's allowed!) the crushed red pepper, jalapeño, and cayenne. The pinch of cinnamon is what really makes this dish in my opinion. To be honest, I use way more than a pinch. And you will be so happy with how these veggies make your house smell.

SERVES 6   HANDS-ON 25 MINUTES   TOTAL 45 MINUTES

2 medium-size sweet potatoes, peeled and cut into 1-inch chunks (about 2 pounds)

3 new potatoes, quartered (about 8 ounces)

2 cups cauliflower florets (about 8 ounces)

1 large tomato, cut into chunks

½ small onion, halved and thinly sliced (about ⅓ cup)

1 small jalapeño chile, seeded and diced

2 garlic cloves, cut in half

2 tablespoons olive oil

½ teaspoon crushed red pepper

¼ teaspoon smoked paprika

⅛ teaspoon ground turmeric

Pinch of ground cinnamon

½ teaspoon kosher salt

¼ teaspoon black pepper

¼ teaspoon cayenne pepper

1. Preheat the oven to 400°F.

2. Toss together the sweet potatoes, new potatoes, cauliflower, tomato, onion, jalapeño, garlic, olive oil, crushed red pepper, paprika, turmeric, cinnamon, salt, black pepper, and cayenne pepper in a large bowl to coat the vegetables in the oil and spices.

3. Transfer to a large lightly greased rimmed baking sheet, spreading in an even layer. Bake anywhere from 20-30 minutes, until golden brown or slightly charred, stirring occasionally.

TIP: Roasting the garlic gives it a milder, sweeter flavor than sautéing it. So feel free to add more cloves of garlic if you wish.

196

Sautéed Spinach

I make sautéed spinach all the time. It's one of Emma's favorites and the dish that she requests every time she comes home from California. It's super good for you. (I was going to list all the health benefits, but there just isn't room. The list is seriously impressive, and I'd suggest looking it up.) I'd also suggest adding this simple recipe to your repertoire as an easy and quick side dish (it's great with the Pan-Roasted Halibut, page 174).

SERVES 4   HANDS-ON 10 MINUTES   TOTAL 10 MINUTES

1. Heat the oil in a large stockpot over medium. Add the garlic and cook 30 seconds. Add the spinach, tossing to coat, and cook 3 to 5 minutes or just until wilted.

2. Remove from the heat, and stir in the lemon juice or vinegar; add salt and black pepper to taste.

TIP: You need a lot of spinach for this dish. One pound of spinach cooks down to about 1 to 1¼ cups.

2 tablespoons olive oil

3 garlic cloves, thinly sliced

2 (16-ounce) packages fresh baby spinach

1½ teaspoons fresh lemon juice (from 1 lemon; apple cider vinegar may be substituted)

AD LIB

If spinach just isn't your thing, or even if it is and you just want to change it up, you can use this exact same recipe and method with asparagus or broccoli.

Sautéed Kale with Parmesan and Toasted Walnuts

I was getting on the tour bus one evening and wanted to take something healthy with me. So I made up this recipe. After a little tweaking, it's turned out to be a delicious go-to. It's also great cold the next day as a salad. I like the depth of flavor the roasted garlic gives this dish, but it would be just as good using two chopped fresh garlic cloves instead.

SERVES 4   HANDS-ON 25 MINUTES   TOTAL 1 HOUR, 30 MINUTES

1 garlic head

2 tablespoons plus 2 teaspoons olive oil

1 small sweet onion, chopped (½ cup)

¼ teaspoon kosher salt

¼ teaspoon smoked paprika

2 bunches Lacinato kale (about 12 ounces), stems removed and chopped

¼ cup chicken stock

1 tablespoon red wine vinegar or apple cider vinegar

⅓ cup golden raisins or dried sweetened cranberries

⅓ cup shaved Parmesan cheese

½ cup chopped toasted walnuts

1. Preheat the oven to 425°F.

2. Cut off the pointed end of the garlic bulb and place the whole bulb on a piece of aluminum foil; drizzle with 2 teaspoons of the olive oil. Fold the foil to seal into a packet. Place the packet, seam side up, in the oven, and bake in the preheated oven for 30 minutes; remove and let cool 20 minutes. Squeeze the pulp from the garlic cloves, and mash it with the tines of a fork.

3. Heat the remaining 2 tablespoons olive oil in a large skillet. Add the onion, and cook for 8 minutes or until tender. Stir in the salt and smoked paprika. Cook for 30 seconds, stirring constantly. Stir in the kale, chicken stock, and 1 tablespoon of the roasted garlic (remaining roasted garlic puree may be kept, covered in olive oil, in the refrigerator up to 1 week). Cook 5 minutes or just until tender.

4. Stir in the vinegar and raisins, tossing to coat. Top with the Parmesan and walnuts just before serving.

Quick Collard Greens

There is a tradition in the South of eating collard greens and black-eyed peas on January 1st to bring good luck and prosperity in the coming year. I love collards any time of year, but these are delicious with the Hoppin' John (page 204). Collards are cooked lots of different ways and everyone usually has a favorite. These are a little spicy, so feel free to adjust the amount of crushed red pepper.

SERVES 6   HANDS-ON 30 MINUTES   TOTAL 40 MINUTES

1. Cook the bacon in a large skillet or Dutch oven 8 minutes or until crisp. Drain, reserving the pan drippings.

2. Stir in the onion, garlic, and crushed red pepper, and cook 5 to 7 minutes or until softened. Stir in the collard greens, tossing to coat. Add the white wine and cook for 2 minutes, or until slightly reduced.

3. Add the chicken broth, sugar, and vinegar, and cook about 10 minutes or just until the collards are tender. Season to taste with salt and pepper. Top with the reserved bacon just before serving.

TIP: If you can't find bagged collard greens and need to use untrimmed ones, just be sure to wash them thoroughly to remove any grit or dirt, and strip the leaves from the stem. You can hold them by the bottom and just run your thumb up the stem to remove, or fold in half and run a sharp knife along the stem.

4 slices bacon, chopped

1 large onion, chopped

2 garlic cloves, minced

¼ to ½ teaspoon crushed red pepper

1 (1-pound) package fresh collard greens, washed and tough stems removed, chopped

¼ cup dry white wine

½ cup chicken broth

2 teaspoons sugar

3 teaspoons apple cider vinegar

Hoppin' John

I had never heard of Hoppin' John until I moved to the South. I love the meaty flavor of black-eyed peas, and made with garlic, shallots, and bacon, this is rich and tasty. It's a Southern tradition to eat black-eyed peas on New Year's Day for luck in the year to come. For a traditional Southern New Year's Day meal, make this Hoppin' John with the Quick Collard Greens (page 203). Add a glass of sweet tea and you have a truly Southern meal!

SERVES 6 TO 8   HANDS-ON 20 MINUTES   TOTAL 1 HOUR, 20 MINUTES

½ pound dried black-eyed
  peas, sorted and rinsed
7½ cups chicken broth
½ pound bacon, chopped
1 medium shallot, minced
  (about 2 tablespoons)
1 tablespoon minced garlic
1 cup uncooked long-grain
  white rice
½ teaspoon kosher salt
¼ teaspoon black pepper
Garnish: chopped green onions

1. Combine the black-eyed peas and 6 cups of the broth in a 3½-quart saucepan, and bring to a boil. Reduce the heat to medium-low and simmer until tender, about 30 minutes. Drain, reserving cooking liquid; set aside.

2. Cook the bacon in the same saucepan until browned and crisp, about 5 to 7 minutes. Remove the bacon, reserving the drippings in saucepan. Add the shallot and garlic, and cook, stirring, until fragrant, 1 minute. Add the rice, salt, and pepper, and cook, stirring, for 1 minute.

3. Measure the reserved cooking liquid, and add enough remaining stock, if necessary, to make 2 cups. Add the stock mixture to the rice mixture, and stir well. Bring to a boil. Cover, reduce the heat, and simmer over medium-low, without stirring, until the liquid is absorbed and the rice is tender, about 20 minutes.

4. Remove from the heat and let stand, covered, 10 minutes. Fluff the rice with a fork, and add the black-eyed peas and bacon, stirring to mix. Garnish with chopped green onions just before serving, if desired.

 TIP: This is great with hot sauce!

Roasted Cinnamon "Harrisburgs" (aka Brussels Sprouts)

When my husband, John, was little, he heard something on the news about Harrisburg, Pennsylvania, while his mom was serving Brussels sprouts, and from that day forward, he has called them Harrisburgs, so we do too at our house.

I must admit I'm relatively new to the Brussels sprouts game. We never had them growing up that I can remember, but I'm kind of obsessed with them now. I try any and every variation I can when we eat out, and I'm always looking for new ways to prepare them. This is one of my favorites and is a perfect side dish for a holiday meal.

SERVES 8   HANDS-ON 30 MINUTES   TOTAL 55 MINUTES

1. Preheat the oven to 400°F.

2. Stir together the Brussels sprouts, 1½ tablespoons of the olive oil, and 1 teaspoon of the salt on a small rimmed baking sheet.

3. Stir together the cubed sweet potatoes, the remaining 1½ tablespoons olive oil, 1½ tablespoons of the maple syrup, cinnamon, and remaining ½ teaspoon salt on another small rimmed baking sheet.

4. Bake the vegetables, stirring and rotating the pans halfway through, for 20 to 25 minutes or until the Brussels sprouts are lightly browned and the potatoes are tender.

5. Stir together the Brussels sprouts, potatoes, pecans, and cranberries in a large bowl. Stir in the remaining 1½ tablespoons maple syrup, and top with the crumbled goat cheese.

TIP: If you have only one large baking sheet you can roast the Brussels sprouts and the sweet potatoes at the same time on the same pan. Just separate them, Brussels sprouts to one side, sweet potatoes to the other.

2 pounds (about 3 cups) small Brussels sprouts, ends trimmed, outer leaves removed, and halved

3 tablespoons olive oil

1½ teaspoons kosher salt

1½ pounds sweet potatoes, peeled and cut into 1-inch cubes (2 medium)

3 tablespoons pure maple syrup

½ teaspoon ground cinnamon

2 cups lightly toasted pecan halves

½ cup sweetened dried cranberries

3 tablespoons crumbled goat cheese

Cilantro, Lime, and Black Bean Rice

This is a great meatless main or side dish. I like it as a side dish with the salmon on page 178, the shrimp tacos on page 181, and the chicken tacos on page 165. It's really versatile so it goes with pretty much any meat dish as well.

SERVES 6   HANDS-ON 15 MINUTES   TOTAL 30 MINUTES

2 cups chicken broth

1 cup uncooked long-grain white rice

½ teaspoon kosher salt

4 garlic cloves, minced

1 tablespoon fresh lime juice or more to taste

1 (15-ounce) can black beans, drained and rinsed

⅓ cup chopped fresh cilantro

Garnishes: cilantro leaves, lime wedges, jalapeño slices

1. Bring the chicken broth, rice, salt, and garlic to a boil over high in a 3½-quart saucepan. Cover, reduce heat to low, and simmer 18 minutes or until the rice is tender and the liquid is just absorbed. Remove the pan from the heat, and fluff the rice with a fork.

2. Stir in the lime juice, black beans, and cilantro. Taste and adjust the seasonings by adding more salt and lime juice to suit your tastes. Transfer to a serving platter, and garnish with cilantro, lime wedges, and jalapeño, if desired.

AD LIB

If you want to make this more of a hearty meatless main dish, fill flour tortillas with this mixture, roll them up, and arrange tightly in a baking dish. Sprinkle the top with 1½ cups shredded cheese, such as Monterey or pepper Jack. Bake at 350°F for 25 to 30 minutes, or until warmed through and the cheese is golden and bubbly. Serve with Avocado Crema (page 251).

Creamy Garlic Pasta with Parmesan Cheese

Well, I'm just going to come out and say it. This is freaking delicious! We have loved this pasta dish for years. It's not the healthiest recipe you'll ever make, but hey, sometimes you just gotta live a little. Remember what I said in my introduction to this book? I try and eat healthy a majority of the time, but when I splurge, I make sure it's worth it. Well, let me tell you, this creamy, cheesy, garlicky (that's a word, right?) DELICIOUS pasta is definitely worth the splurge, so enjoy each and every bite!

SERVES 4   HANDS-ON 20 MINUTES   TOTAL 20 MINUTES

1. Melt the butter in a large Dutch oven over medium. Add the garlic, and sauté for 30 seconds, stirring constantly. Add the salt, pepper, and chicken broth and bring to a boil over high. Add the pasta, and cook 4 minutes, stirring occasionally, or just until al dente (do not drain).

2. Reduce the heat to medium, and stir in the Parmesan cheese. Remove from the heat, and stir in the cream. Garnish with chopped fresh parsley, if desired, and serve immediately.

2 tablespoons butter
4 garlic cloves, minced
¼ teaspoon kosher salt
½ teaspoon black pepper
3 cups chicken broth
8 ounces uncooked angel hair pasta
1 cup grated Parmesan cheese
¾ cup heavy cream
Garnish: chopped fresh parsley

AD LIB

There is none. It's perfect just the way it is! It's a good side for grilled chicken or topped with chopped grilled chicken.

Pumpkin Cornbread with Cinnamon-Honey Butter

I love the fall twist on this cornbread as a side to soup or the Quick Collard Greens on page 203. I prefer it without the honey butter. But with the honey butter it almost becomes a dessert. And it's delicious with your morning cup!

SERVES 6 TO 8   HANDS-ON 25 MINUTES   TOTAL 50 MINUTES, INCLUDING BUTTER

1 cup all-purpose flour

1 cup plain yellow cornmeal

1 teaspoon baking powder

½ teaspoon baking soda

½ teaspoon kosher salt

½ teaspoon ground cinnamon

½ teaspoon ground ginger

¼ teaspoon ground nutmeg

¼ teaspoon ground cloves

½ cup packed light brown sugar

¼ cup unsalted butter, melted

1 cup canned pumpkin

½ cup sour cream

2 large eggs

Cinnamon-Honey Butter (recipe follows)

1. Preheat the oven to 375°F.

2. Whisk together the flour, cornmeal, baking powder, baking soda, salt, cinnamon, ginger, nutmeg, and cloves in a large bowl. Make a well in the center. Stir together the brown sugar, butter, pumpkin, sour cream, and eggs in a small bowl. Add the pumpkin mixture to the flour mixture, stirring just until combined. Pour into a greased 8- x 8-inch baking pan.

3. Bake 25 to 30 minutes or until a wooden pick inserted in the center comes out clean. Let cool completely on a wire rack. Serve with the Cinnamon-Honey Butter.

Cinnamon-Honey Butter

½ cup butter, softened

⅓ cup honey

¼ cup powdered sugar

1 teaspoon ground cinnamon

Beat the butter with a mixer at high speed until creamy. Reduce speed to low, and add the honey, powdered sugar, and cinnamon. Beat at high speed until light and fluffy, about 2 minutes. Makes about ½ cup

 TIP: This is a delicious bread to wrap up to give to friends and neighbors during the holidays.

MARTINA'S KITCHEN MIX

DESSERTS

SO, YOU'VE SERVED SOME ENTICING APPETIZERS as the first course. You've made a delicious main course and complemented it with a loaded salad or a couple of colorful side dishes. Now it's time to bring it home!

Biting into something sweet at the end of a meal is heavenly for most people and a common way to finish a meal. I'm more of a savory person than a sweets person, so I usually have no problem skipping dessert (though I do have a personal superstition that if someone is having a birthday celebration, it's bad luck not to eat a piece of the birthday cake!). As a matter of fact, I sometimes forget how much people love desserts and have to remind myself to make one when I have company!

The sugar addiction in this country is a bit of an epidemic. My husband is one of those sugar-addicted people. I got into the habit of limiting access to sugar for my three daughters as they were growing up, so I'm not really the kind of mom who had a plate of warm cookies waiting when they got home from school. But, I'll say it again, I do believe in balance and sometimes I crave something sweet like everyone else. When I do eat dessert, the indulgence needs to really be "worth it," so I was pretty picky about the recipes that I created for this chapter. Of course I enlisted the help of my band and crew by taking treats out on the road each week for them to "taste test." They were only too happy to help out and were quite up for the challenge. I guess you could say that these desserts are "road crew approved," so if you ever find yourself cooking for a bunch of roadies, you can be confident they will love pretty much any of these desserts!

I will admit that I do really enjoy ice cream. I love the coldness and creaminess of it. My favorite ice-cream flavor at the moment is salted caramel. I became a little obsessed with finding a couple of cookie recipes that would make a great ice cream sandwich. (My family was extremely happy that I tested so many cookie recipes!) The Thin and Crispy Chocolate Chip Cookies (page 240) and the Peanut Butter-Chocolate Chip-Oatmeal Cookies (page 236) are excellent with a scoop of ice cream sandwiched in between. And the Individual No-Bake Chocolate-Cherry Cheesecakes with Biscoff Crust (page 218) just might be my favorite dessert of all.

So go ahead and splurge now and then! These desserts are definitely worth it.

Individual No-Bake Chocolate-Cherry Cheesecakes with Biscoff Crust

This cheesecake is fun (who doesn't want their own personal portion of heaven?), rich, decadent, and delicious. And it is just as good (or maybe even better) the next day — so feel free to prepare it a day ahead.

SERVES 8   HANDS-ON 40 MINUTES   TOTAL 4 HOURS, 55 MINUTES, INCLUDING TOPPING

20 Biscoff cookies (such as Lotus)
2 tablespoons granulated sugar
3 tablespoons butter, melted
1 cup dark chocolate chips
2 (8-ounce) packages cream cheese, softened
½ teaspoon vanilla extract
¼ teaspoon kosher salt
1¼ cups heavy cream
½ cup powdered sugar

CHERRY TOPPING
1 (12-ounce) package frozen dark, sweet pitted cherries
¼ cup sugar
1 tablespoon cornstarch
1 tablespoon orange liqueur (such as Grand Marnier, or orange juice may be substituted)
⅛ teaspoon kosher salt
Whipped cream, for topping

1. Process the cookies and granulated sugar in a food processor for 30 seconds or until finely ground. Add the butter; pulse 8 to 10 times or until combined. Press the mixture into bottoms of 8 (8-ounce) serving glasses (or small canning jars).

2. Microwave the chocolate in a medium-size, microwave-safe bowl 50 seconds to 1 minute or until melted and smooth, stirring after 30 seconds. Let cool slightly.

3. Beat the cream cheese with a mixer at medium speed 2 to 3 minutes until fluffy. Add the vanilla, salt, and melted chocolate, beating at low speed until well blended.

4. Beat the whipping cream until foamy; gradually add the powdered sugar, beating until soft peaks form. Fold the whipped cream into the chocolate mixture. Spoon into the glasses. Cover and chill 4 hours or until set.

5. For the topping, cook the cherries and sugar in a small saucepan over medium 5 minutes or just until the sugar dissolves. Stir the cornstarch with 1 tablespoon water in a small bowl. Stir into the cherries; cook, stirring frequently, 5 minutes or just until thickened. Remove from the heat. Stir in the orange liqueur (or orange juice) and salt. Let cool.

6. Top each serving with a layer of whipped cream and the Cherry Topping to serve.

AD LIB

Change the flavor of this cheesecake by using gingersnaps in place of Biscoff cookies. Omit the chocolate chips (or not) and top with Cranberry Orange Relish (page 253).

County Fair Orange Cake

*You never know where you're going to find a great recipe. I tasted this backstage
at the County Fair in Owensville, Missouri—and on my birthday nonetheless!
One bite and I was blown away. So much so, I went back and asked if they
would share the recipe for this book. Not only did they share the recipe, but they
sent some cake to my tour bus so I could take it home! I don't eat desserts much
because I really don't have a big sweet tooth and would rather save my calorie
intake for cheese (call me crazy!). I cook healthy most of the time and avoid
prepared ingredients, but every once in awhile I like to eat the way I grew up
eating . . . back when boxed cake mixes and instant pudding were pantry staples.
I think that's why I loved this cake so much—it just transported me back home.*

SERVES 16   HANDS-ON 20 MINUTES
TOTAL 2 HOURS, 30 MINUTES, INCLUDING COOLING TIME AND GLAZE

1. Preheat the oven to 350°F. Grease and flour 2 (9- x 5-inch) loaf pans.

2. Stir the cake and pudding mixes in a large bowl. Add the orange juice, oil, eggs, and zest; beat on low with a mixer at low speed to combine. Scrape down sides. Beat at medium for 4 minutes.

3. Pour the batter into the prepared pans. Bake 45 minutes or until a wooden pick inserted in center comes out clean. Cool in pans on a wire rack 15 minutes; remove from pans to wire rack. Cool completely, about 1 hour. Transfer to a platter. Pour warm Orange Glaze over the cake.

1 (15.25-ounce) package yellow
   cake mix
1 (3.5-ounce) package lemon
   instant pudding mix
¾ cup orange juice
½ cup vegetable oil
4 large eggs
2 teaspoons lemon zest
Orange Glaze (recipe follows)

Orange Glaze

½ cup sugar
⅓ cup orange juice

¼ cup butter
1 teaspoon orange zest

Cook the sugar, orange juice, and butter in a saucepan over medium, stirring, until the butter is melted. Cook 2 more minutes, and remove from the heat; stir in the orange zest.

TIP: You can also make this in a 10-inch Bundt pan (as pictured). Bake for the same amount of time.

Fresh Apple Cake with Homemade Caramel Sauce

I first served this on a crisp fall evening. We were eating outside and the air was just starting to get that chill that signals autumn has arrived. The comments that I heard after my family and dinner guests took the first couple of bites were: "This tastes like apple cider in cake form" and "No, it tastes just like a caramel apple" and "I think this tastes just like fall." I like that the cake isn't overly sweet, because the sauce is. So, if super-sweet is not your thing, you can leave off the caramel sauce. I drizzled, okay ladled, warm caramel sauce over the top and added a scoop of vanilla ice cream because . . . well, why not? But the next morning I had a piece of the cake sans sauce with my cup of coffee. On its own, it was light and equally delicious.

SERVES 16   HANDS-ON 30 MINUTES
TOTAL 1 HOUR, 10 MINUTES, INCLUDING SAUCE

½ cup butter, softened

2 cups sugar

2 large eggs

2 cups (about 2 apples) grated
   unpeeled Granny Smith apple

2 cups all-purpose flour

1½ teaspoons baking soda

2 teaspoons ground cinnamon

1½ teaspoons ground cloves

¼ teaspoon kosher salt

1 cup chopped walnuts
   (optional)

Homemade Caramel Sauce
   (page 261)

Whipped cream or ice cream
   (optional)

1. Preheat the oven to 350°F.

2. Beat the butter with a mixer at medium speed until fluffy; gradually add the sugar, beating well. Add the eggs, 1 at a time, beating just until blended after each addition. Add the apple, beating just until blended.

3. Whisk together the flour, baking soda, cinnamon, cloves, and salt; add to the butter mixture, and mix just until blended. Stir in the walnuts, if desired.

4. Pour into a lightly greased 13- x 9-inch baking pan. Bake 30 to 35 minutes or just until a wooden pick inserted in the center comes out clean. Let cool on a wire rack 10 minutes. Serve with Homemade Caramel Sauce and, if desired, whipped cream or ice cream.

 You can use most any kind of apple. Gala or Red Delicious work great too.

Banana Cake with Cream Cheese Frosting

This moist and delicious cake is not overly sweet. It's amazing with the Cream Cheese Frosting (duh!), but if you're watching your sugar intake, I like it just as well without frosting. If you take it to a potluck, you might as well print the recipe on cards and keep them in your pocket because everyone is going to ask you for it! This cake tastes even better the day after it's made, so it's a great make-ahead party recipe. And, yes, the low oven temperature is correct!

SERVES 16   HANDS-ON 25 MINUTES
TOTAL 1 HOUR, 25 MINUTES, INCLUDING COOLING TIME AND FROSTING

1. Preheat the oven to 275°F. Grease a 13- x 9-inch baking pan.

2. In a small bowl, mix the mashed bananas and lemon juice.

3. Beat the butter with a mixer at medium speed until creamy. Gradually add the sugar, beating well. Add the vanilla and eggs, 1 at a time, beating well after each addition.

4. Combine the flour, baking soda, and salt in a bowl. Add the flour mixture to the butter mixture, alternately with the buttermilk. Beat at low speed until blended after each addition, scraping down bowl as needed. Stir in the banana mixture. Pour the batter into the prepared pan.

5. Bake 1 hour or until a wooden pick inserted in center comes out clean. Cool completely in pan on a wire rack (or freeze 45 minutes for faster cooling).

6. For the frosting, beat the butter and cream cheese with a mixer at medium-high speed until creamy, 3 minutes. Gradually add the powdered sugar at low speed until blended. Increase the speed to medium. Add the vanilla and salt. Beat 1 minute until light and fluffy. Spread the frosting on top of the cake.

1½ cups mashed ripe bananas (about 3 bananas)
2 teaspoons lemon juice
¾ cup butter, softened
2 cups sugar
2 teaspoons vanilla extract
3 large eggs
3 cups all-purpose flour
1½ teaspoons baking soda
¼ teaspoon table salt
1½ cups buttermilk

CREAM CHEESE FROSTING
½ cup butter, softened
1 (8-ounce) package cream cheese, softened
3½ cups powdered sugar
1 teaspoon vanilla extract
Pinch of kosher salt

DON'T KNOCK IT 'TIL YOU TRY IT

This crazy concoction is another "treasure" from my childhood! I could never get any of my friends to try this when I was growing up, despite my assurances that it was so delicious. And that's pretty much been the case as an adult as well, but luckily my kids love it! So I asked Ava what to say about this recipe and she said, "This sounds like an odd recipe, but it's actually really good, so don't judge it until you've tried it." My thoughts exactly!

Banana Mayo "Thing"

SERVES 10   HANDS-ON 10 MINUTES   TOTAL 10 MINUTES

1 large ripe banana

2 teaspoons good-quality mayonnaise
  or Miracle Whip

Ground cinnamon, to taste

Peel the banana, and slice in half lengthwise. Spread cut sides with the mayonnaise, and sprinkle with cinnamon.

TIP: Good-quality mayo is important here. My favorite is Duke's mayonnaise.

Biscotti Trio

Biscotti, which means "twice-baked" in Italian, are crunchy oblong cookies traditionally dunked in drinks. They're crunchy and full of flavor without being too sweet. I've come up with three of my favorite spins. Serve these with coffee or tea for a quick bite in the morning, as a nice addition to a brunch menu, or the Old World way: with coffee or port at the end of a dinner party. (Yep, dunk them right into the wine!) These keep up to two weeks in an airtight container.

MAKES 2 DOZEN   HANDS-ON 30 MINUTES   TOTAL 1 HOUR, 5 MINUTES

4 tablespoons butter, softened

1 cup sugar

2 large eggs

2 cups all-purpose flour

½ teaspoon baking powder

½ teaspoon baking soda

¼ teaspoon kosher salt

½ cup whole almonds, chopped

⅓ cup dried cherries

½ teaspoon almond extract

1. Preheat the oven to 350°F.

2. Beat the butter and sugar with a mixer at high speed until thick and pale, about 2 minutes. Add the eggs, 1 at a time, beating until blended.

3. Whisk together the flour, baking powder, baking soda, and salt in a small bowl. Beat the flour mixture with the butter mixture at low speed until blended. Add the almonds, dried cherries, and almond extract and beat until blended.

4. Divide the dough in half. Turn out onto a greased baking sheet. Shape each portion into an 8- x 3-inch log (about ¾ inch thick). Arrange logs 2 inches apart on the baking sheet.

5. Bake 25 minutes or until lightly browned. Let logs cool 10 minutes on a wire rack. Reduce oven temperature to 300°F.

6. Slice each log on the diagonal with a serrated knife into 12 (¾-inch) slices. Arrange slices, cut sides down, on the greased baking sheet. Bake slices 10 minutes, turn, and bake 10 more minutes (biscotti will be slightly soft in the center, but will harden as they cool). Transfer from the baking sheet to cool completely on a wire rack.

 Wrap these in a cellophane gift bag tied with ribbon for a sweet hostess or holiday gift.

variations

Cranberry-Orange-Almond Biscotti: Prepare the recipe as directed, adding 1 tablespoon orange zest to the batter in Step 2 and substituting ⅓ cup sweetened dried cranberries for the cherries. Makes 2 dozen

Pistachio-Cranberry Biscotti: Prepare the recipe as directed, substituting ½ cup chopped pistachios for the almonds, ⅓ cup sweetened dried cranberries for the cherries, and 1 teaspoon vanilla extract for the almond extract. Makes 2 dozen

Pistachio Lemon Drop Cookies

This is one of the most unusual cookie recipes I've made. I adapted it from a Martha Stewart recipe that intrigued me because it was so different. Well, it is different and absolutely delicious. I can never eat just one. These are great with a cup of coffee or espresso in the afternoon.

MAKES 1 ½ DOZEN COOKIES   HANDS-ON 20 MINUTES   TOTAL 30 MINUTES

1. Preheat the oven to 325°F.

2. Beat the egg white and salt with a mixer fitted with the whisk attachment on high speed until stiff peaks form. Reduce the speed to medium, and add the nuts and brown sugar, beating 1 minute. Add the flour and lemon juice, beating until combined.

3. Drop by tablespoonfuls about 2 inches apart onto parchment paper-lined baking sheets. Bake the cookies in the preheated oven, in batches, until the edges are golden, 10 to 12 minutes. Let cool on pans on wire racks.

TIP: Usually I'm all about making recipes ahead as most recipes get better with time. Not this one. I'm just being honest. These are meant to be eaten up the day you make them, which, fortunately, isn't hard to do!

1 large egg white
Pinch of coarse sea salt
1 cup finely chopped salted, toasted pistachios
1 cup packed light brown sugar
1 tablespoon all-purpose flour
½ teaspoon fresh lemon juice

No-Bake Peanut Butter-Chocolate Cookies

When I was in high school, we had the best "lunch ladies" around: Thelma, Betty, and Virginia. I went to a small school where everything was made from scratch. The whole school rejoiced when we had No-Bake Cookies. I have added peanut butter to these over the years because I love peanut butter-chocolate combo. When I took these out on the road for my band and crew to "taste test," the consensus was unanimous that this recipe must make it into the book!

MAKES 1½ DOZEN COOKIES   HANDS-ON 20 MINUTES   TOTAL 50 MINUTES

½ cup butter

1¾ cups sugar

½ cup milk

¾ cup creamy peanut butter

2 teaspoons vanilla extract

¼ teaspoon kosher salt

3 cups uncooked quick-cooking oats

1 cup (6 ounces) milk or dark chocolate chips

1. Line 2 baking sheets with wax or parchment paper.

2. Melt the butter in a 3½-quart saucepan over medium. Stir in the sugar and milk; bring to a boil. Boil for 1½ minutes.

3. Remove from the heat, and immediately stir in the peanut butter, vanilla, salt, and oats, stirring to combine. Add the chocolate, stirring just until combined.

4. Drop the dough by rounded tablespoonfuls onto the prepared baking sheets. Let the cookies stand 30 minutes or until set.

 TIP: Two 4-ounce dark chocolate bars, chopped, may be substituted for the milk or dark chocolate chips.

Peanut Butter-Krispie Cookies

———

I have a thing for peanut butter and swoon over a good peanut butter cookie. If there is a plate of peanut butter cookies in catering when I'm on the road, guaranteed I'm having one (or two)! This recipe has a little extra goodness with the addition of the rice cereal, which gives it a nice crunchy texture. Use any type of chocolate chips that you wish. Milk chocolate, semisweet, dark . . . whatever you have on hand.

MAKES ABOUT 2 DOZEN HANDS-ON 30 MINUTES TOTAL 1 HOUR

1. Preheat the oven to 350°F.

2. Whisk together the flour, baking soda, and salt in a small bowl.

3. Beat the butter and sugars with a mixer at medium speed until pale and fluffy, about 3 minutes. Add the egg; beat until well blended. Add in the vanilla and peanut butter. Reduce the speed to low, beating until combined.

4. Gradually add the flour mixture, and beat until just combined. Stir in the cereal and chocolate chips.

5. Shape the dough into 1½-inch balls and place 1 inch apart on parchment-lined baking sheets. Flatten the balls gently with a spatula or the tines of a fork.

6. Bake the cookies, rotating the baking sheets halfway through, until centers are firm and edges are lightly browned, about 12 minutes. Transfer the cookies to a wire rack to cool completely.

1 cup all-purpose flour

½ teaspoon baking soda

¼ teaspoon kosher salt

½ cup unsalted butter, softened

¼ cup granulated sugar

¾ cup packed light brown sugar

1 large egg

1 teaspoon vanilla extract

1 cup crunchy peanut butter

1 cup crisp rice cereal (such as Rice Krispies)

1¼ cups dark chocolate chips

Peanut Butter-Chocolate Chip-Oatmeal Cookies

I've always loved cookies that are loaded with a lot of stuff, and these have a handful of my faves—chocolate, peanut butter, and rolled oats for good measure. Oh, and shelled whole peanuts for a nice crunch. These cookies are so full of flavor, it's definitely hard to have just one.

MAKES 6 DOZEN   HANDS-ON 40 MINUTES   TOTAL 1 HOUR, 5 MINUTES

3 cups uncooked old-fashioned rolled oats

⅓ cup all-purpose flour

1 teaspoon baking soda

1 teaspoon baking powder

½ teaspoon kosher salt

1 cup unsalted butter, room temperature

1 cup packed light brown sugar

1 cup granulated sugar

½ cup creamy peanut butter

2 large eggs

1 teaspoon vanilla extract

2 cups salted whole peanuts

2 cups semisweet chocolate chips

1. Preheat the oven to 350°F. Stir together the oats, flour, baking soda, baking powder, and salt in a large bowl.

2. Beat the butter with a mixer at medium speed. Add the sugars, and beat until fluffy, about 2 minutes. Add the peanut butter, and beat 1 minute. Add the eggs, 1 at a time, beating after each addition. Stir in the vanilla.

3. Reduce the speed to low, and beat in the oats mixture just until combined. Add the peanuts and chocolate chips.

4. Drop by heaping tablespoonfuls 2 inches apart on parchment-lined baking sheets.

5. Bake, in batches, rotating the sheets halfway through until the edges are golden brown and just set, 10 to 11 minutes.

6. Let cool on the baking sheets on a wire rack 5 minutes. Transfer the cookies to the wire rack to cool completely.

variation

Ice-Cream Sandwich Cookies: Scoop 3 cups softened vanilla ice cream onto flat sides of half of cookies; top with remaining cookies, flat sides down. Place in ziplock plastic freezer bags, and freeze at least 1 hour.

Thin and Crispy Chocolate Chip Cookies

I've said it before: I'm not the best baker. But these turned out perfectly crisp, thin, and absolutely delicious. They are great with a glass of ice-cold milk or crumbled up on top of vanilla ice cream.

MAKES 3 DOZEN   HANDS-ON 35 MINUTES   TOTAL 1 HOUR, 45 MINUTES

2¼ cups all-purpose flour

½ teaspoon baking soda

1¼ cups unsalted butter, room temperature

1¼ cups granulated sugar

¾ cup packed light brown sugar

1 teaspoon kosher salt

2 teaspoons vanilla extract

2 large eggs

¼ cup water

2 cups semisweet chocolate chips

1. Preheat the oven to 350°F.

2. Whisk together the flour and baking soda in a bowl.

3. Beat the butter and sugars with a stand mixer fitted with the paddle attachment, or mix with a handheld mixer, at medium speed until pale and fluffy, about 3 minutes. Reduce the speed to low. Add the salt, vanilla, eggs, and water, and beat until combined, about 1 minute. Add the flour mixture, and beat until just combined. Stir in the chocolate chips.

4. Drop heaping teaspoon-size balls of dough about 3 inches apart on parchment-lined baking sheets. Bake the cookies, in batches (6 cookies per batch), rotating the baking sheets halfway through until golden brown, 12 to 14 minutes. Let cool on the baking sheets on wire racks 1 to 2 minutes. Transfer the cookies to wire racks to cool completely.

TIP: It's important to follow these directions with this cookie. The dough is thinner than normal cookie dough, so don't make them too big.

AD LIB

Add a little cinnamon to the batter to change it up. Sprinkle the cookies with a tiny bit of sea salt before baking for a sweet-and-salty combo.

Chocolate Flourless Cake

And here you have it: My go-to dinner party dessert. I've made this so many times and it always turns out perfectly—rich, moist, and decadent. I love serving small slices with a dollop of whipped cream or vanilla ice cream on the side. Try this recipe without the cinnamon for classic chocolate or add the cinnamon to give it more of a Mexican chocolate note.

SERVES 10 TO 12   HANDS-ON 20 MINUTES
TOTAL 2 HOURS, 30 MINUTES, INCLUDING COOLING

1. Preheat the oven to 350°F.

2. Lightly butter the bottom and sides of a 10-inch springform pan. Dust bottom and sides with the cocoa, shaking to remove excess.

3. Combine the bittersweet chocolate and butter in a large bowl. Microwave for 1 minute or until completely melted and smooth, stirring at 30-second intervals. (Alternately, melt in a small metal bowl set over a saucepan of simmering water, stirring until smooth.) Let cool slightly. Whisk in the sugar and cinnamon, if desired. Whisk in the eggs, 1 at a time, whisking well after each addition. Sift the remaining 1 cup cocoa over the mixture, and whisk until just combined.

4. Pour the batter into the prepared pan, and bake 30 to 35 minutes or just until barely set. Transfer to a wire rack; let cool for 10 minutes. Run a knife around the edges to loosen, and remove sides. Remove to a serving platter, and let cool completely. Dust with additional cocoa or powdered sugar. Serve with ice cream or sweetened whipped cream, if desired.

1 cup unsweetened cocoa plus more for dusting
8 ounces bittersweet chocolate, chopped
1 cup unsalted butter
1½ cups sugar
⅛ teaspoon ground cinnamon (optional)
6 large eggs
Vanilla ice cream or sweetened whipped cream, for serving

AD LIB

I always sweeten my homemade whipped cream with a little powdered sugar and a touch of vanilla extract.

EVERY COOK HAS A FAVORITE BASIC RECIPE (or a handful) that they whip up again and again because it tastes amazing or can be used in multiple ways . . . or it's both those things so it becomes a standard on their cooking playlist. I find there are two camps of cooks when it comes to such recipes. On one side there are those who keep their best recipe tricks a closely guarded secret (or if they do share, it seems they always leave a little something out so that it's never quite as good when someone else makes it). In the other camp, there are cooks who create something so delicious that they cannot wait to share it with others and will happily share the recipe with anyone who loves it as much. Obviously, I'm in that latter camp or I wouldn't be publishing this cookbook!

While I was testing recipes for this book, I came up with some really great ones that I found to be so versatile that I just couldn't put them in any one chapter or lump them with a single recipe. I worried if I did that, you would make only the dressing, or sauce, or whatever it might be, in that one particular way. Most of the recipes in this chapter can be used in multiple ways. I've noted throughout the book where I use these favorites, but I'm hoping you will use your imagination and come up with new ways of your own, and even add them to recipes you've made many times as a way to update, or put a new spin on, one of your family favorites.

Some of these recipes make unique host or housewarming gifts. I have a friend who gives edible homemade gifts for Christmas every year. I always look forward to getting them. I think a jar of the Homemade Caramel Sauce (page 261) in this chapter would be appreciated by most anyone. It keeps in the fridge and is delicious on ice cream and on the Fresh Apple Cake in the Desserts chapter (page 222), or you could just stir it into your morning coffee in place of sweetener. The Pesto Butter (page 259) can be frozen and pulled out at the last minute to add flavor to plain pasta or fish. I can think of a hundred ways (well, maybe not a hundred, but close) to use the Green Goddess Dressing (page 255). And the Garlic Bread (page 258) goes fast in our house!

So enjoy my favorite basics in this chapter and think of them as great "go-to" basics to add to your cooking repertoire.

Homemade Taco Seasoning

I used to always use packaged taco seasoning until I realized making your own was easy and healthier. This mix seasons one pound of ground beef. Double it, or triple it even, and keep it in an airtight container, so you always have it on hand.

MAKES 3½ TABLESPOONS   **HANDS-ON 15 MINUTES**   **TOTAL 15 MINUTES**

1 tablespoon chili powder

1½ teaspoons ground cumin

1 teaspoon sea salt

1 teaspoon black pepper

½ teaspoon smoked paprika

¼ teaspoon garlic powder

¼ teaspoon onion powder

¼ teaspoon crushed red pepper

¼ teaspoon dried oregano

Whisk the chili powder, cumin, salt, pepper, paprika, garlic powder, onion powder, crushed red pepper, and oregano in a small bowl. Store in an airtight container up to 6 months.

Southwest Citrus Rub

This is a great all-purpose rub for chicken, shrimp, or veggies. Use ½ teaspoon ground cumin for the cumin seeds in a pinch, and chipotle chili powder in place of the regular chili powder for a spicy, smoky kick.

MAKES ABOUT ¼ CUP   **HANDS-ON 10 MINUTES**   **TOTAL 10 MINUTES**

1 teaspoon cumin seeds

2 teaspoons brown sugar

1½ teaspoons chili powder

½ teaspoon paprika

½ teaspoon dried oregano

⅛ teaspoon cayenne pepper

1 teaspoon kosher salt

½ teaspoon lime zest

2 tablespoons lime juice

1½ tablespoons olive oil

1. Toast the cumin seeds in a small cast-iron skillet over medium 2 minutes or just until fragrant. Remove from the heat; let cool. Crush the seeds with a mortar and pestle or in a ziplock bag with a small heavy skillet or rolling pin.

2. Stir together the crushed cumin, brown sugar, chili powder, paprika, oregano, cayenne, salt, lime zest and juice, and olive oil. Cover and chill until ready to use.

AD LIB

Beyond tacos, the Homemade Taco Seasoning is a great rub for most any grilled meats. Use it to season ground beef for a taco soup. Just simmer in vegetable broth with diced tomatoes and green chiles, corn, and pinto beans. Serve topped with sour cream and a bit of chopped cilantro or my Avocado Crema on page 251.

Grilled Pineapple Salsa

Grilling the ingredients gives this salsa smoky flavor. If you don't have a grill, just chop the pineapple, onion, and pepper and grill them in a grill pan on the stove until they get a slight char.

MAKES 3 CUPS   HANDS-ON 25 MINUTES   TOTAL 25 MINUTES

½ fresh cored pineapple, cut into
   3 (¾-inch-thick) rounds
1 small red onion, quartered
1 small red chile pepper, or jalapeño,
   thinly sliced

2 tablespoons chopped fresh cilantro
½ teaspoon lime zest
1 tablespoon lime juice
½ teaspoon chili powder
Kosher salt and black pepper

1. Preheat a charcoal grill to medium-high (about 450°F). Grill the pineapple, onion, and red pepper, turning occasionally, 8 to 10 minutes or until charred. Let cool, chop, and transfer to a bowl.

2. Stir in the cilantro, lime zest and juice, and chili powder. Season with salt and pepper. Serve immediately or chill until ready to serve.

Avocado Crema

This versatile sauce adds flavor to the Chili Lime Chicken Tacos (page 165). Top a baked potato or fish with it, or dunk chicken fingers in it.

MAKES 1 CUP   HANDS-ON 15 MINUTES
TOTAL 4 HOURS, 15 MINUTES, INCLUDING 4 HOURS CHILLING

1 medium-size ripe avocado, peeled
   and chopped
½ cup sour cream (or plain Greek
   yogurt)
2 tablespoons mayonnaise

1 small garlic clove, chopped
1 tablespoon lime juice
1 tablespoon chopped fresh cilantro
1 to 2 teaspoons Mexican hot sauce
Kosher salt and black pepper

Process the avocado, sour cream, mayonnaise, garlic, lime juice, cilantro, and hot sauce in a food processor 30 seconds until smooth, scraping down sides as needed. Season to taste with salt and pepper. Cover; chill up to 4 hours.

Martina's Gremolata

My spin on the versatile Italian topping adds texture and flavor to a variety of recipes. It's easy to prepare, and once you make it, you'll want to keep some on hand for sprinkling on everything from roasts and soups to fish, green beans, and even the asparagus (page 186). It's a must on top of my Very Green Broccoli Soup (page 127).

MAKES ABOUT ¼ CUP   HANDS-ON 10 MINUTES   TOTAL 10 MINUTES

1 tablespoon finely chopped lightly toasted pine nuts or hazelnuts

1 teaspoon lemon zest

1½ tablespoons fine, dry breadcrumbs

1½ tablespoons finely chopped fresh flat-leaf parsley

⅛ teaspoon kosher salt

Small pinch of freshly ground black pepper

Stir together the pine nuts, lemon zest, breadcrumbs, parsley, salt, and pepper in a small bowl. Cover and refrigerate up to 3 days.

TIP: Make sure your parsley is washed to remove grit, and dried well. It's good to do this several hours before you make the gremolata, if possible, so that it can be completely dry.

AD LIB

So many ways to use gremolata! Mix it into a vinaigrette, or use it to top a salad, especially arugula and shaved Parmesan. Add some oil to it and use it as a rub for chicken breasts before grilling. Replace 2 tablespoons of the breadcrumbs in your meatloaf mixture with ¼ cup of gremolata for bright flavor.

Cranberry Orange Relish

———

This is a great relish for the holidays, but also nice as an unexpected
"extra" touch with roasted pork. It smells divine and is so easy to make.

MAKES 1 CUP   HANDS-ON 10 MINUTES   HANDS-ON 10 MINUTES

1 (12-ounce) bag fresh cranberries
½ cup sugar
¾ cup port

2 teaspoons orange zest
2 tablespoons freshly squeezed
    orange juice

Cook the cranberries and sugar in a small saucepan over medium 5 minutes
or just until sugar melts. Stir in the port and cook over medium-low 10 to
15 minutes or until thickened and the cranberries begin to pop. Remove from
the heat and stir in the orange zest and orange juice. Let cool completely.
Cover and refrigerate until ready to serve.

Classic Vinaigrette

———

A good vinaigrette is really all about proportions. As a rule of thumb, you want a ratio of three parts oil to one part acid. Adjust the formula accordingly to suit your tastes to make it more or less tangy. You also can change the types of vinegar, citrus juice, or oil—try toasted walnut or avocado in place of olive oil. Add grated citrus zest, a bit of minced garlic, or a spoonful of chopped fresh herbs—or all three. Once you master a basic vinaigrette, you can create countless riffs. I make a big batch of vinaigrette in a glass jar to use on salads for days.

MAKES ABOUT 1 CUP   HANDS-ON 5 MINUTES   TOTAL 5 MINUTES

1 small shallot, minced

1 garlic clove, smashed

½ teaspoon Dijon mustard

1 teaspoon chopped fresh thyme

¼ teaspoon kosher salt

Freshly ground black pepper

¼ cup sherry vinegar

½ cup extra-virgin olive oil

Combine the shallot, garlic, mustard, thyme, salt, and pepper in a medium bowl. Whisk in the vinegar. Add the oil in a slow, steady stream, whisking until smooth.

variation

Balsamic-Sherry Vinaigrette: Use half aged balsamic vinegar and half sherry vinegar for a sweet depth of flavor.

Citrus Vinaigrette

MAKES ABOUT 1 CUP   HANDS-ON 5 MINUTES   TOTAL 5 MINUTES

1 small shallot, minced
½ teaspoon lemon zest
¼ teaspoon kosher salt
Freshly ground black pepper
1 teaspoon honey

2 tablespoons freshly squeezed
   lemon juice
2 tablespoons unseasoned
   rice vinegar
½ cup avocado oil

Combine the shallot, zest, salt, pepper, and honey in a medium bowl. Whisk in the lemon juice and rice vinegar. Add the oil in a slow, steady stream, whisking until smooth.

variation

Citrus-and-Herb Vinaigrette: Add 1 to 2 teaspoons chopped fresh, tender herbs like chives, mint, parsley, basil, or a blend of several, to this vinaigrette.

Green Goddess Dressing

This is terrific as a salad dressing, an alternative to cocktail sauce for chilled shrimp, a topping for baked potatoes, stirred into mashed potatoes, or as a dip for asparagus on a vegetable tray. The possibilities are endless.

MAKES 1⅓ CUPS   HANDS-ON 15 MINUTES   TOTAL 15 MINUTES

¾ cup plain Greek yogurt
⅓ cup mayonnaise
2 tablespoons buttermilk (optional)
½ cup fresh parsley leaves
¼ cup chopped fresh chives
1 tablespoon chopped fresh basil
2 teaspoons chopped fresh tarragon

1 garlic clove
2 teaspoons lemon zest
1 tablespoon fresh lemon juice
1 teaspoon Worcestershire sauce
½ teaspoon kosher salt
¼ teaspoon black pepper

Process the yogurt, mayonnaise, buttermilk, if desired, parsley, chives, basil, tarragon, garlic, lemon zest, lemon juice, Worcestershire, salt, and pepper in a food processor 30 seconds or until smooth. Cover and refrigerate until ready to serve.

Garlic Bread

When my family hears I'm making spaghetti or lasagna for supper, I always hear "make garlic bread!" We pretty much devour it. So I always double this and make two loaves.

SERVES 8 TO 10   **HANDS-ON 15 MINUTES**   **TOTAL 40 MINUTES**

2 teaspoons finely chopped garlic

¼ teaspoon kosher salt

4 tablespoons butter, softened

1 tablespoon extra-virgin olive oil

1 (16-ounce) loaf French or Italian bread

1. Preheat the oven to 350°F.

2. Place the chopped garlic in a small bowl; add the salt to the bowl. Smash together the salt and garlic, pressing with the back of a spoon to make a paste. Stir in the butter and olive oil.

3. Cut the bread diagonally into 1-inch-thick slices, without cutting through to the bottom. Spread the slices evenly with the garlic butter.

4. Wrap in heavy-duty aluminum foil, and bake 15 minutes.

5. Open the foil and bake until the bread is crusty on top, 10 more minutes. Serve warm.

TIP! You can make loaves of this bread ahead and freeze, wrapped in foil. Just pop it out of the freezer and add 10 to 12 minutes to the cooking time. If thawed, cook as directed.

AD LIB

You can add a little chopped fresh parsley to your butter and garlic mixture to make it pretty.

Pesto Butter

You will want to make up a batch of this flavorful butter to have in the freezer and on hand because it can be used in many ways. Stir into hot cooked pasta. Top a baked potato. Add it to grilled chicken. Toss with grilled shrimp. For an easy appetizer, spread on toasted baguette slices, and top with diced or roasted tomatoes. And, of course, it's delicious on the Pan-Roasted Halibut (page 174).

MAKES ½ CUP   HANDS-ON 20 MINUTES   TOTAL 20 MINUTES

½ cup unsalted butter, softened

1 cup fresh basil leaves

¼ cup grated Parmesan cheese

2 tablespoons toasted pine nuts

1 garlic clove, peeled

½ teaspoon kosher salt

¼ teaspoon crushed red pepper

Process the butter, basil, Parmesan, pine nuts, garlic, salt, and crushed red pepper in a food processor 30 seconds or until smooth. Shape the butter into a 6-inch log on a sheet of plastic wrap; roll up, twisting ends to secure. Refrigerate until 30 minutes before using.

Chipotle Sauce

MAKES ½ CUP   HANDS-ON 5 MINUTES   TOTAL 5 MINUTES

½ cup mayonnaise or sour cream

2½ teaspoons minced canned chipotle peppers in adobo sauce

1½ teaspoons honey

1 teaspoon lime juice

Whisk together the mayonnaise, peppers, honey, and lime juice in a small bowl. Season to taste with salt and black pepper.

Homemade Caramel Sauce

This sauce is so good and so easy you will never buy another jarred caramel sauce again. It's delicious over ice cream, stirred into hot coffee, or drizzled on top of my Fresh Apple Cake (page 222). Keep it refrigerated up to one week after you make it. Just be sure to warm it up before serving.

MAKES 1 CUP   **HANDS-ON 10 MINUTES**   **TOTAL 10 MINUTES**

1 cup packed light brown sugar

½ cup half-and-half

4 tablespoons butter

Pinch of kosher salt

Cook the sugar, half-and-half, butter, and salt in a small saucepan over medium-low for 5 to 7 minutes, whisking slowly until thickened. Remove from the heat, and let cool slightly before serving.

TIP: A jar of this sauce is a sweet hostess or housewarming gift. Attach a tag noting its many uses.

MY PLAYLIST

It's always hard for me to make a playlist that's going to be published because I feel like people take it to be my "favorite songs of all time." These are some of my favorites, but I was really just going for a vibe and a feeling I like to experience when I cook in the kitchen. Otherwise, I would have a lot more sad songs here, believe me. But the only reason to cry in the kitchen should have something to do with chopping onions. So I put together songs that give me energy, that I can sing and dance to, and then we end with more of a mellow vibe. Enjoy!

Hallelujah I Love Her So....Ray Charles

Baby I Love You....Aretha Franklin

Rehab....Amy Winehouse

Soldier....Gavin DeGraw

Son of a Preacher Man....Dusty Springfield

Will It Go Round In Circles....Billy Preston

Signed, Sealed, Delivered (I'm Yours)....Stevie Wonder

September....Earth, Wind & Fire

Small Town....John Mellencamp

Start Me Up....The Rolling Stones

Pride and Joy....Stevie Ray Vaughan

Stay With Me....Faces

Bye Bye Blackbird....Joe Cocker

Love Is Strange....Mickey & Sylvia

Ladyfingers....Herb Alpert & The Tijuana Brass

Throwing It All Away....Genesis

One Big Love....Patty Griffin

Right Down the Line....Gerry Rafferty

Mr. Blue Sky....ELO

Mrs. Robinson....Simon & Garfunkel

Ode to Billie Joe....Bobbie Gentry

Gentle On My Mind....Glen Campbell

Me and Bobby McGee....Kris Kristofferson

Crazy Love....Van Morrison

Easy....The Commodores

Goodbye Yellow Brick Road....Elton John OR Sara Bareilles

Heavenly Day....Patty Griffin

Martina's Menu Mix

BRUNCH IDEAS

All of these brunch menus are meant to be buffet style so guests just grab a little bit of this and that. Or all of it! As always, feel free to simplify.

Southern Brunch

Blackberry-Lemon Gin and Tonic *or* Blackberry Julep *(page 40)*

Smoked Gouda Pimiento Cheese on crostini *(page 63)*

Flavia's Deviled Eggs *(page 46)*

Hash Brown Breakfast Casserole with Tomato Gravy *(page 26)*

Green Beans with Goat Cheese and Warm Bacon Dressing *(page 190)*

Cheddar Biscuits with Bacon *(page 25)*

Banana Cake with Cream Cheese Frosting *(page 225) or* Grandma's Cinnamon Rolls *(page 34)*

Spring Brunch

Sparkling Grapefruit Mimosas *(page 57)*

Avocado Toast with Corn-and-Tomato Salsa *(page 19)*

Yogurt cups topped with blueberries and Cherry-Orange-Almond Granola *(page 16)*

Springtime (or Anytime) Quiche *(page 20)*

Romaine Salad with Buttermilk Parmesan Dressing *(page 95) or* Boston Lettuce Simple Salad *(page 100)*

County Fair Orange Cake *(page 221) or* Grandma's Cinnamon Rolls *(page 34)*

Fall Brunch

Baked French Toast with Pecan Crumble and Blackberry-Maple Syrup *(page 32)*

Platter of bacon or breakfast sausage

Flavia's Deviled Eggs *(page 46)* (or big bowl of eggs scrambled with chives and sage)

Fried Cornmeal "Mush" *(page 30)*

Mexican Brunch

Grapefruit Margaritas *(page 58)*

Avocado, Cucumber, and Red Pepper Salsa with chips *(page 50)*

Grilled Shrimp Tacos *(page 181)*

Chipotle Chicken Taco Salad *(page 119)*

Chocolate Flourless Cake *(page 243)* (add cinnamon for a Mexican chocolate flair)

New Year's Day Brunch

Irish Coffee *(page 86)*

Hoppin' John *(page 204)*

Quick Collard Greens *(page 203)*

Fruit salad

Pumpkin Cornbread with Cinnamon-Honey Butter *(page 212)*

DINNER IDEAS

These can be as elaborate or as easy as you wish. I've included a signature cocktail, appetizer, and dessert for most of the menus, which leans more to a dinner party vibe. But feel free to simplify for a satisfying family meal.

Healthy-ish Dinner #1

Marinated Goat Cheese with Lemon and Herbs *(page 67)*

Pan-Roasted Halibut with sautéed grape tomatoes *(page 174)*

Sautéed Spinach *(page 197) or* Risotto with Asparagus, Peas, and Basil *(page 150)*

County Fair Orange Cake *(page 221)*

Healthy-ish Dinner #2

Grilled Sweet Peppers with Goat Cheese and Herbs *(page 45)*

Slow-Roasted Garlic-Dijon Salmon *(page 178)*

Creamy Garlic Pasta with Parmesan Cheese *(page 211)*

Cranberry, Avocado, and Spinach Salad with Orange-Poppy Seed Dressing *(page 106)*

Strawberries and blueberries (with fresh whipped cream)

Classic and Comfy Dinner

Blackberry-Lemon Gin and Tonic *(page 40)* or
Vodka Limeade Cooler *(page 49)*

Baked Olive Cheese Dip *(page 78)* (served with crackers
and/or chips for spreading or dipping)

Chicken and Potatoes with Roasted Lemon
and Rosemary Sauce *(page 154)*

Sautéed Spinach *(page 197)* or
Roasted Asparagus with Lemon, Parmesan, and Garlic
(page 186) (or just plain sautéed asparagus drizzled with
olive oil and sprinkled with salt and pepper)

Romaine Salad with Pear, Smoked Blue Cheese,
and Candied Pecans *(page 99)* or
Boston Lettuce Simple Salad *(page 100)*

Peanut Butter-Chocolate Chip-Oatmeal
Ice-Cream Sandwich Cookies *(page 236)*

Italian Dinner

Negroni *(page 73)*

Whipped Feta Crostini with Roasted Garlic,
Tomatoes, and Herbs *(page 42)*

Antipasti tray (assortment of meat such as salami,
prosciutto, cheese, olives, breadsticks, crackers)

Meatballs and Red Sauce *(page 74)*

Boston Lettuce Simple Salad *(page 100)*

Garlic Bread *(page 258)*

Individual No-Bake Chocolate-Cherry
Cheesecakes with Biscoff Crust *(page 218)*

Mexican Dinner

Grapefruit Margaritas *(page 58)*

Shrimp and Chorizo with Latin Flavors *(page 68)*

Chili Lime Chicken Tacos with Grilled Pineapple
Salsa and Avocado Crema *(page 165)*

Cilantro, Lime, and Black Bean Rice *(page 208)*

Grilled corn on the cob

Banana Cake with Cream Cheese Frosting *(page 225)*

LUNCH

Lunch is a great time to catch up with friends and family. It can be easier, in a way, than a dinner party and is often overlooked as an entertaining option. In addition to obvious lunches like the Greek Grilled Chicken, Cucumber-Tomato Salad, and Tzatziki Sauce (page 160), which is great for a desktop lunch bowl, I've put together some tasty lunch menu options here for you.

"Salad" Sampler Lunch with Girlfriends
(Mix and match or make all of them!)

Blackberry-Lemon Gin and Tonic *(page 40)* or
Vodka Limeade Cooler *(page 49)*

Chipotle Chicken Taco Salad *(page 119)*

Kale Caesar Salad with Quinoa and Chicken *(page 112)*

Broccoli and Cauliflower Salad *(page 96)*

Watermelon, Cucumber, and Tomato Salad
wtih Feta and Fresh Herbs *(page 92)*

Pistachio Lemon Drop Cookies *(page 231)*

Alfresco Spring Lunch

Grapefruit Margaritas *(page 58)*

Grilled Pineapple Salsa with chips *(page 251)*

Blackened Fish Taco Bowls *(page 177)*

Banana Cake with Cream Cheese Frosting *(page 225)*

Cozy Winter Lunch

Whiskey Smash *(page 81)*

Smoked Gouda Pimiento Cheese *(page 63)*
(with breadsticks or crackers)

Quick-and-Easy White Bean and
Baby Greens Stew *(page 128)*

Toasted baguette or
Garlic Bread *(page 258)*

Fresh Apple Cake with
Homemade Caramel Sauce *(page 222)*

METRIC EQUIVALENTS

The recipes that appear in this cookbook use the standard United States method for measuring liquid and dry or solid ingredients (teaspoons, tablespoons, and cups). The information in the following charts is provided to help cooks outside the U.S. successfully use these recipes. All equivalents are approximate.

METRIC EQUIVALENTS FOR DIFFERENT TYPES OF INGREDIENTS

A standard cup measure of a dry or solid ingredient will vary in weight depending on the type of ingredient. A standard cup of liquid is the same volume for any type of liquid. Use the following chart when converting standard cup measures to grams (weight).

Standard Cup	Fine Powder (ex. flour)	Grain (ex. rice)	Granular (ex. sugar)	Liquid Solids (ex. butter)	Liquid (ex. milk)
1	140 g	150 g	190 g	200 g	240 ml
³⁄₄	105 g	113 g	143 g	150 g	180 ml
²⁄₃	93 g	100 g	125 g	133 g	160 ml
¹⁄₂	70 g	75 g	95 g	100 g	120 ml
¹⁄₃	47 g	50 g	63 g	67 g	80 ml
¹⁄₄	35 g	38 g	48 g	50 g	60 ml
¹⁄₈	18 g	19 g	24 g	25 g	30 ml

USEFUL EQUIVALENTS FOR DRY INGREDIENTS BY WEIGHT

(To convert ounces to grams, multiply the number of ounces by 30.)

1 oz	=	¹⁄₁₆ lb	=	30 g
4 oz	=	¹⁄₄ lb	=	120 g
8 oz	=	¹⁄₂ lb	=	240 g
12 oz	=	³⁄₄ lb	=	360 g
16 oz	=	1 lb	=	480 g

USEFUL EQUIVALENTS FOR LENGTH

(To convert inches to centimeters, multiply the number of inches by 2.5.)

1 in				=	2.5 cm			
6 in	=	¹⁄₂ ft		=	15 cm			
12 in	=	1 ft		=	30 cm			
36 in	=	3 ft	=	1 yd	=	90 cm		
40 in				=	100 cm	=	1 m	

USEFUL EQUIVALENTS FOR LIQUID INGREDIENTS BY VOLUME

¹⁄₄ tsp						=	1 ml	
¹⁄₂ tsp						=	2 ml	
1 tsp						=	5 ml	
3 tsp	=	1 Tbsp		=	¹⁄₂ fl oz	=	15 ml	
		2 Tbsp	=	¹⁄₈ cup	=	1 fl oz	=	30 ml
		4 Tbsp	=	¹⁄₄ cup	=	2 fl oz	=	60 ml
		5¹⁄₃ Tbsp	=	¹⁄₃ cup	=	3 fl oz	=	80 ml
		8 Tbsp	=	¹⁄₂ cup	=	4 fl oz	=	120 ml
		10²⁄₃ Tbsp	=	²⁄₃ cup	=	5 fl oz	=	160 ml
		12 Tbsp	=	³⁄₄ cup	=	6 fl oz	=	180 ml
		16 Tbsp	=	1 cup	=	8 fl oz	=	240 ml
		1 pt	=	2 cups	=	16 fl oz	=	480 ml
		1 qt	=	4 cups	=	32 fl oz	=	960 ml
						33 fl oz	=	1000 ml = 1 l

USEFUL EQUIVALENTS FOR COOKING/OVEN TEMPERATURES

	Fahrenheit	Celsius	Gas Mark
Freeze water	32°F	0°C	
Room temperature	68°F	20°C	
Boil water	212°F	100°C	
Bake	325°F	160°C	3
	350°F	180°C	4
	375°F	190°C	5
	400°F	200°C	6
	425°F	220°C	7
	450°F	230°C	8
Broil			Grill

INDEX

IT TAKES A VILLAGE! I'D LIKE TO GIVE SPECIAL THANKS TO:

My editor, Katherine Cobbs. I'm so glad I got to do a second book with you. Thanks for answering my thousands of texts and emails and for your boundless encouragement, guidance, and talent.

Jason Wallis, David McClister, Paden Reich, Caviar & Bananas, Woodland Wine Merchant, Little Gourmand, Taylor Colson Horton, Tami Hardeman, Melanie Shelley, Lindsey Doyle, and Ali Benner for the beautiful photos. Melissa Clark for the lovely book design.

Lyda Jones Burnette and the Food Studios staff for making sure all my ducks were in a row when it came to the recipes. I really appreciate all of your hard work.

Coren Capshaw and all at Red Light Management. Daniel Miller and Chris Ferren, for steering the ship.

Danielle Costa, Kourtney Sokmen, Anja Schmidt, and everyone at Meredith SIM Books. This is going to be a fun ride!

My band and crew for being my "taste testers." Sharon Joines for the wonderful Orange Cake recipe.

John, Delaney, Emma, and Ava for your patience as I talked incessantly about food and recipes, for eating everything I cooked while researching this book, and for all of your love and support always. I love you.